Discover
ARIZONA!

by Rick Harris

**GOLDEN
WEST** ☼
PUBLISHERS

Acknowledgement

The following persons have in one way or another contributed to the production of this work:

Kirk McRight, Paul Postma, Dave Eichentopf, Bonnie Sanders, Sharon Lewis, Mike Biewener, Rodger Hartgrave, Spencer Clifton, Barbara Hickey, Amy Zamar, Greg Goodson, Bridget Watson, Mike Warren and Tom German. Lastly, special kudos to Marty Smith.

Without all that they have done, this book would not have been possible.

MILEAGE ESTIMATES MAY VARY

Mileage can be altered somewhat when one is traveling on a dirt road. It is not uncommon to go to a site one time and then another, only to find that the projected and the actual mileage can differ at times by five to ten miles. In most instances, the author has used topographical maps to gauge mileage.

Cover photo by Shayne Fischer

Library of Congress Cataloging-in-Publication Data

Harris, Richard L.

Discover Arizona! / by Richard L. Harris with maps by the author.

Includes index.

1. Arizona—Description and travel—Guide-books. 2. Historic sites—Arizona—Guide-books. 3. Natural history—Arizona—Guide-books. I. Title.

F809.3.H36 1991	917.9104'53—dc20	90-23407
ISBN 0-914846-52-3 (pbk.)		CIP

Printed in the United States of America

Golden West Publishers
4113 N. Longview
Phoenix, AZ 85014, USA
(602) 265-4392

Contents

(Maps appear on the second page of each chapter.)

CAVEAT (WARNING)

The sites depicted on the maps in this book lie in areas which may be under the jurisdiction of the State of Arizona, the federal government or various Indian tribal authorities. Laws and regulations for each of these jurisdictions differ with respect to the type of collecting activities permitted.

For the amateur collector, the State of Arizona permits collecting of arrowheads, coins or bottles (see Arizona Revised Statutes §41-841.— Archaeological discoveries); the federal government permits the collection of paleontological remains, coins, bullets, and unworked minerals and rocks (Title 16, U.S. Code, Section 470, and following, 43 Code of Regulations (CFR), Part 7). A serious amateur is urged to read these statutes and regulations in full.

Arrowheads located on federal lands are placed in a separate category. While casual collecting of arrowheads lying on the surface of the ground is not subject to criminal enforcement, the arrowheads are nonetheless considered as federal property and discretion is advised in collecting.

With respect to Indian lands, the visitor or collector is urged to check with the applicable tribal authority.

If in doubt as to the jurisdiction of a site and the activity permitted, the reader is urged to look and enjoy, but don't touch.

Physical hazards may be encountered in visiting areas of *Discover Arizona,* particularly old mining localities. Land ownerships and road conditions change over the years. Readers should take proper precautions and make local inquiries, as author and publisher cannot accept responsibility for such matters.

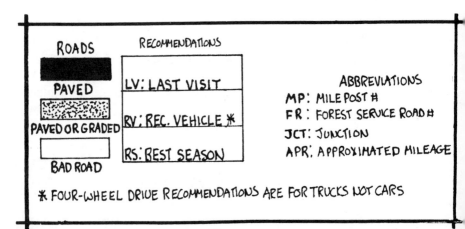

Introduction

Arizona is a magnificent state. With something for everyone. And, while I am sitting here wondering how to adequately describe this magnificence, I realize that no poem, song, picture, or words could ever do justice to Arizona.

That is something that can only be realized when you leave the city behind for a week or a month. Then, if you are very lucky, Arizona will reveal herself to you, as she has to a select few.

Centuries before Europeans set foot in the Southwest, American Indians had arrived. With them came a special reverence for nature.

Today, for most people, Arizona is property, the land is ownership and market value. Trees are only here to provide us with paper and firewood. Wild animals are a nuisance—they run into our cars and bend the fenders. Mountains only hamper our road building.

The Arizona I seek is far away from the highways and therefore has little market value. Subdivisions would have sprung up where I like to go, but the water table is just too low, and bringing in electricity would cost a fortune.

Federal laws protect wild life, as well as my beloved Indian ruins. If it were not for the nesting eagles, the Verde would be lined from Jerome to Phoenix with condominiums!

Some of you have written to me asking whether it is wise of me to disclose these sites. Whether they will be destroyed by the inconsiderate, by treasure hunters, by those who have no regard for nature, the past or themselves.

Rest assured. All of the sites we have revisited since publication of *Explore Arizona* are in the same condition they were when we first visited them. Only time and the elements have taken their toll.

This is not to say that damage will never happen. I have seen plenty of sites that have been ruined or completely destroyed by vandals. To this day, national monuments are still being vandalized and spray-painted. Nothing is immune from jerks who get their jollies from screwing things up for everyone else.

However, the only people who purchase my books are people like you. We are much like the Indians who came before, in that our love for nature and Arizona outweighs any destructive tendencies we may have.

Since 1986, my friends and I have been exploring the Arizona outback, from Kayenta to Clarkdale, from Tucson to Tuzigoot. We now present another fifty sites for you to discover and explore.

Drive out to the waterfalls, caves, Indian ruins, canyons, lakes and streams. And, I will, too! You can bet on it!

Rick Harris

1. Marsh Pass

Most people who venture to this far corner of Arizona do so in search of the famed ruins of Betatakin and Keet Seel. If ruins are your interest, then Marsh Pass is the place for you.

Starting from the Tsegi Trading Post, you hike west into the canyon. Within three miles you will reach the Swallow Nest Ruin, a well-preserved favorite that we have visited a number of times. Take special note of the wooden scaffolding—still in place—which is some 700 years old.

From the Swallow Nest Ruin, follow a barely discernible trail for about four miles to the next canyon. Here you will see the unexcavated ruin known locally as Batwoman House. Almost as large as Keet Seel, and more accessible, this ruin holds a hoard of artifacts.

Be forewarned that any artifacts you may find, including arrowheads, are not to be removed from these ruins. While you can collect arrowheads in other parts of the state, you cannot from the Navajo Nation. Take your pictures and your memories and nothing else!

SPECIAL NOTES:

Photograph these ruins in winter and you will not be sorry. However, I would advise caution, because wet snow can be treacherous.

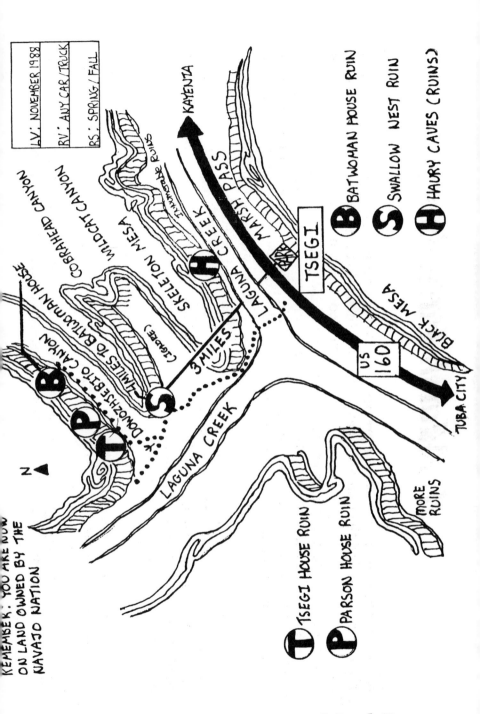

LV: NOVEMBER 1988
RV: ANY CAR/TRUCK
BS: SPRING/FALL

REMEMBER: YOU ARE NOW ON LAND OWNED BY THE NAVAJO NATION

N

CORRAHEAD CANYON

WILDCAT CANYON

DOWOZHIE BITO CANYON

CORRAHEAD CANYON

4 MILES TO BATWOMAN HOUSE

SKELETON MESA

Unnameable Ruins

(Craters)

3 MILES

LAGUNA CREEK

LAGUNA CREEK

LAGUNA MARSH PASS

LAGUNA CREEK

KAYENTA

TSEGI

US 160

BLACK MESA

TUBA CITY

MORE RUINS

B BATWOMAN HOUSE RUIN

S SWALLOW NEST RUIN

H HAIRY CAVES (RUINS)

T TSEGI HOUSE RUIN

P PARSON HOUSE RUIN

Marsh Pass

(7)

2. *Kinlichee Pueblo*

Set handsomely among groves of juniper and pinon one will find the ruin of Kinlichee Pueblo.

The importance of this particular ruin is that it was one of the last settlements abandoned by the Hopi Indians before they migrated to the now famous mesas, some 400 years ago.

Most of the eighty rooms of this pueblo were excavated in the early part of this century, but there are enough artifacts remaining to give the viewer an idea of what life was like in eleventh-century Arizona.

As a side note, we were told by local inhabitants that there was a ghost who frequented the ruin on nights of a full moon. Two weeks later we made the decision to camp the creek and see if this was true. It was right after dusk when we heard strange noises and the distant sound of breaking glass. Could it be the ghosts of Kinlichee?

Rather, it was the very live souls of two homeboys who requested a ride into nearby Window Rock.

So much for legends!

SPECIAL NOTES:

I have been collecting Kachina dolls from this region for years. As a consummate consumer of these treasured artworks, I will testify that the Kachina is of Hopi origin. Only copies can be bought from other nearby tribes.

Jewelry is the forte of the Navajo. This is where they excel. Buy your Kachinas from the Hopi and your jewelry from the Navajo for investment and for the sake of authenticity.

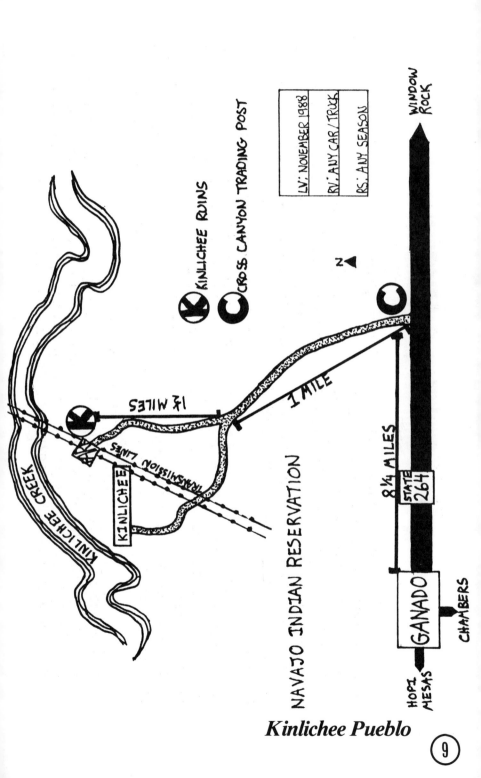

Kinlichee Pueblo

⑨

3. Awatovi Ruins

Just outside Keams Canyon and high upon Antelope Mesa stand the ruins of Awatovi, a village of the Hopi that once ranked second in importance to the religious community of Oraibi.

But, while Oraibi prospered and grew, Awatovi met a violent death at the hands of fellow Hopis.

In 1700, a group of warriors from the surrounding villages swept down on the helpless inhabitants of Awatovi and massacred the entire population.

The reason for this action: the people who dwelt in this village had chosen to accept the foreign Christian religion and forsake their own.

Even to this day, traditionalistic Hopis will not walk upon Antelope Mesa because the Hopi are a people of peace, and here and only here, Hopi killed Hopi. They regard it with disgrace.

When you stand before Awatovi, you can feel the spirits of those long gone. You will even feel as if they wish you to leave. It is an eerie feeling, but not so imposing as you might feel is you were to remove artifacts. Even in Hopiland, you are permitted to take photographs and memories, but nothing else.

SPECIAL NOTES:

You will detect a seemingly silent hostility when dealing with the natives and you might wonder why. If you act like a tourist and behave like a conqueror, you can expect to be treated like an idiot. These are proud people. Treat them with the same respect you give yourself and there will be no problem, no hostility, and probably the best time of your life!

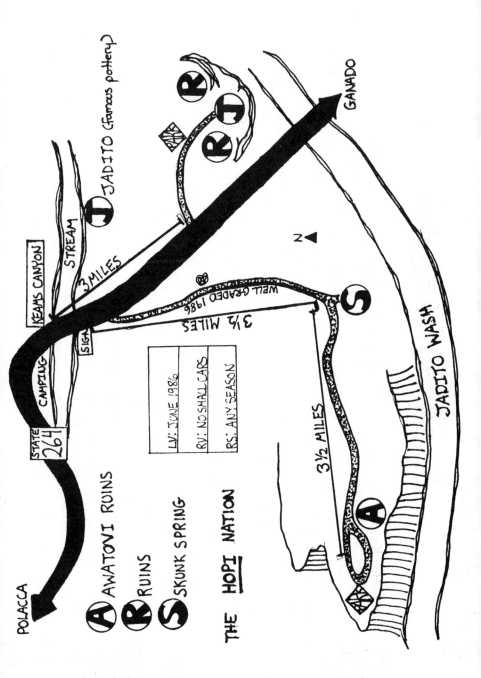

Awatovi Ruins

4. Five-Mile Wash

The next time you find yourself traveling between Cameron and the Grand Canyon, you may want to take a small detour into the stark desert that is your constant cussed companion.

I am talking about that area which appears to hold little or nothing of interest. However, to the right (north), and just beyond that distant desolate mound, you will find the unexplored, pristine remains of an ancient forest.

Petrified as they are, trees that once ringed a primordial lagoon beg a closer look. That is what you will find here! Your own petrified forest awaits!

Take nothing of those items that abound here, lest you are willing to take on the burden of one hefty fine.

SPECIAL NOTES:

These logs fell some million years ago, covered with Triassic period slime. That was actually 160 million years ago, give or take a million. Anyhow, silica-rich sediments impregnated the logs, converting them to stone over the eons. Simply stated, they turned into massive megaliths of agate which have lasted to this day.

Please don't remove even the tiniest particle of this matter. You see, at one time this was the last place on earth where you could find petrified tree stumps. There are no more left to find here because thoughtless people took these oddities. You will find none!

And, so that others might enjoy what is left of the site, I ask you to take nothing more than pictures and leave nothing more than footprints.

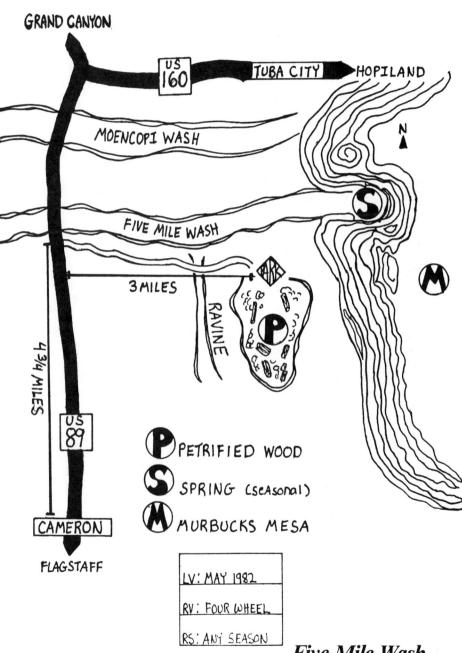

GRAND CANYON

US 160

TUBA CITY → HOPILAND

MOENCOPI WASH

N

FIVE MILE WASH

S

M

3 MILES

RAVINE

P

4 3/4 MILES

US 89

P PETRIFIED WOOD

S SPRING (seasonal)

M MURBUCKS MESA

CAMERON

FLAGSTAFF

LV: MAY 1982

RV: FOUR WHEEL

RS: ANY SEASON

Five-Mile Wash

⑬

5. Grand Falls

If you are considering a trip to Navajo-land, I would suggest that you postpone until the White Mountains have had a chance to shed their gift on this region.

With this in mind, eventually you will see a breathtaking sight at this locale when the runoff flows down the Little Colorado River and cascades over Grand Falls!

Higher than Niagara—and much more impressive—Grand Falls will only reveal herself during the month of July. When rain hits the White Mountains, it makes a beeline to Grand Falls, and then—well—beauty overtakes your senses.

Contrasting hues of salmon-red waters drape the ebony lava and sunflower limestone to create a distortion of colors. All made by nature, all for you! It is a painter's paradise, with or without canvas.

As you travel the road past Merriam Crater to Grand Falls, you may take note of a change in the black landscape. You will have come in on a light dirt road, and suddenly you'll be riding lava cinders. Grand Falls was created by this same ashen flow when nearby Rodin Crater overflowed and forever altered the path of our favored Little Colorado. Hence, Grand Falls!

SPECIAL NOTES:

Do not wear a luau shirt or funky shorts when you come out here. And, for your own sake, do not travel to Grand Falls in a travel home. Abide by these suggestions lest you leave here carrying fake native goods.

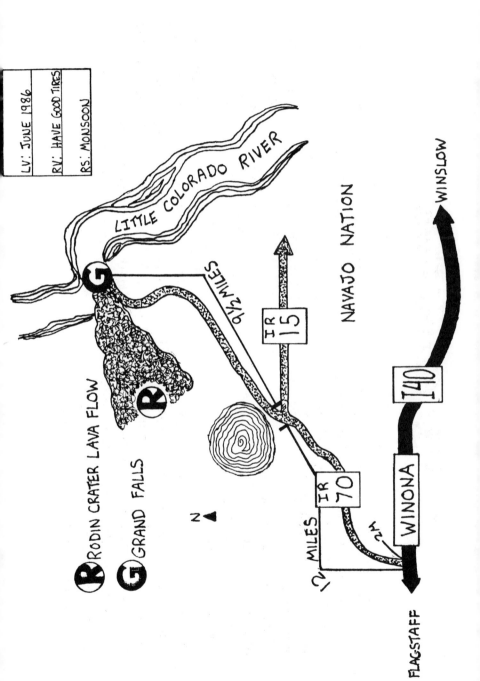

LITTLE COLORADO RIVER

NAVAJO NATION

WINSLOW

I40

WINONA

FLAGSTAFF

IR 15

IR 70

9½ MILES

2 MILES

2M

RODIN CRATER LAVA FLOW

GRAND FALLS

R RODIN CRATER LAVA FLOW

G GRAND FALLS

N

LV: JUNE 1986
RV: HAVE GOOD TIRES
RS: MONSOON

Grand Falls

15

6. White Hills Excursion

Quite frankly, ghost towns disappoint me. It seems that every ghost town that we are told of as "in good condition" turns out to be little more than a few foundations.

Such was the case once again when we visited the ghost town of White Hills. We found a lot of foundations, one or two walls and nothing else.

So, why write about it? I am glad you asked that question. Normally, we would have gone on to Vegas to forget our troubles and, in the process, create more.

You see, while the town of White Hills has been relegated to dust, the tailings from the mines which once supported this community still abound with their own variety of treasures.

If you can avoid the temptation of these thoroughly dangerous mine shafts and focus your attention on those little nuggets of turquoise and azurite in the dumps, then your trip might just pay bigger than Vegas.

And, if you are an antique buff, you may just want to poke around the many mounds which abound in the site.

All in all, STAY OUT OF THOSE SHAFTS because they are too old—the kind where the slightest vibration will cause an interior avalanche.

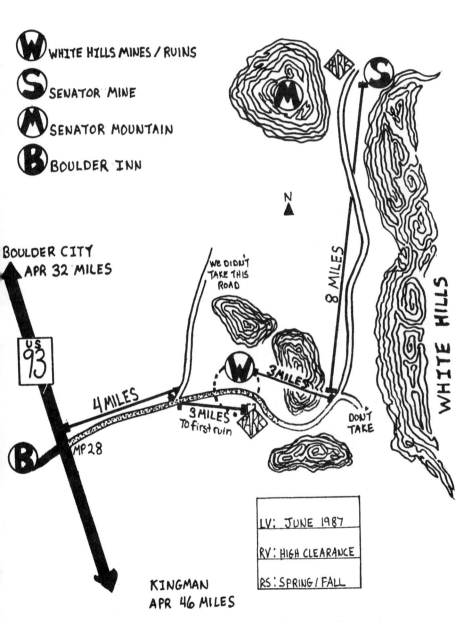

W WHITE HILLS MINES / RUINS

S SENATOR MINE

M SENATOR MOUNTAIN

B BOULDER INN

BOULDER CITY
APR 32 MILES

WE DIDN'T
TAKE THIS
ROAD

US 93

N

8 MILES

WHITE HILLS

4 MILES

W 3 MILES

3 MILES
TO first ruin

DON'T
TAKE

MP 28

B

KINGMAN
APR 46 MILES

LV: JUNE 1987

RV: HIGH CLEARANCE

RS: SPRING / FALL

White Hills Excursion

⑰

7. Chloride Roundabout

Chloride, Arizona, is not a place you would normally think of for a vacation time, and that is a shame because these people—the ones who live in Chloride—are some of the friendliest I have ever met.

Check this town out and check out this tour . . .

Alright, antique freaks, this trip is just for you! Understand that the Chloride area has been mined for decades. People have been tripping around this area for more than a hundred years.

The area is loaded with the assorted sundries that people have used. In fact, you can find a horde of antique dealers in Chloride. They sell items for far less than you will pay in Phoenix or Tucson.

Yet, if you want to find your own, paying for only your gas, drive this dirt road and look for the mines.

Stay out of the mine shafts. These mine shafts are dangerous and can cost you your life! Just ask anyone in Chloride!

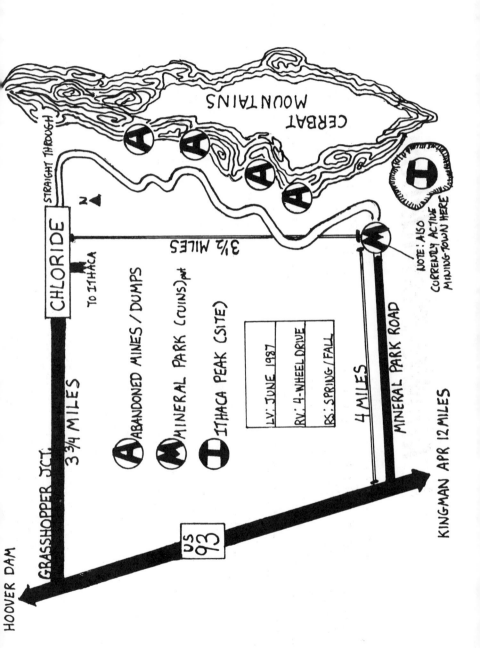

Chloride Roundabout

8. Chavez Pass Ruins

I have never written to my readers about a site that has not already been pot-hunted. The archeologists say that once a ruin has been disturbed it is no longer any use to them.

If this is so, then what is the big deal? I might also add that I try to write only about ruins on federal and state land. FEDERAL: that is you and me. STATE: that is you and me again.

We have the right to visit any of these sites on our MUTUAL land, just so that we abide by the law or laws which have been passed to protect these sites for future generations to view. Enough said.

The ruins of Chavez Pass have been pot-hunted for decades. There really is little or nothing left for other pot hunters here. My interest in the site stems from the apparent fact that it was a fortified site and possibly a trading center between northern and southern natives at one time.

If you look closely at what pottery types still remain in the form of shards, you will notice Hohokam intermingled with Anasazi! Arrowheads—the only things you can legally take from this site—surround the entire pass.

Not to discourage you from visiting Chavez Pass, but I should warn any potential pot hunter that the ground has been laced with tiny pellets that give off a radio signal if they are broken, thus alerting the proper authorities of a potential crime taking place at the site.

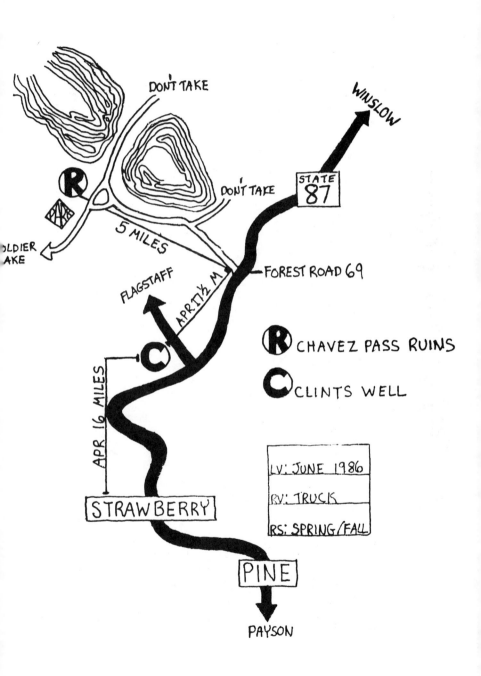

DON'T TAKE

WINSLOW

DON'T TAKE

STATE 87

R

SOLDIER LAKE

5 MILES

FLAGSTAFF

FOREST ROAD 69

APR 17½ M

R CHAVEZ PASS RUINS

C CLINTS WELL

C

APR 16 MILES

STRAWBERRY

LV: JUNE 1986

RV: TRUCK

RS: SPRING/FALL

PINE

PAYSON

Chavez Pass Ruins

9. *The Verbalitis Ruin*

This ruin is very special to me, even though it is not that impressive.

Most of the walls are tumbled, stray beer cans litter the site, and pothunters have dug as many holes as the gophers. It's not an impressive ruin at all.

Nevertheless, the air is always good atop the peak, and the clouds choose to twist and curl into the most fantastic of shapes when they pass overhead.

From here you can see forever in any direction, with clarity, and I suppose that is what I love about the ruin.

More importantly, it also reminds me of a man who once could see with great clarity everything that was around him. He gave that ability to everyone who knew him. I knew him. His name was Victor Verbalitis.

"Verb" was a friend, as well as a teacher of mine. I owe ninety-nine per-cent of my artistic insight to his insights. Let me say that he brought out a lot of my own self which was hidden.

On July 10, 1986, he was killed in a freak accident of nature while doing what he did best, helping students to see and appreciate the natural world around them. He will be sorely missed.

Chances are that Verb never saw this ruin in his lifetime, although he did enjoy ruins and he did enjoy studying ancient pottery forms. Yet, a part of my sight is eternally linked to that of Victor Verbalitis. Through my eyes, he has seen the ruin and I believe he approves the name I have given to it.

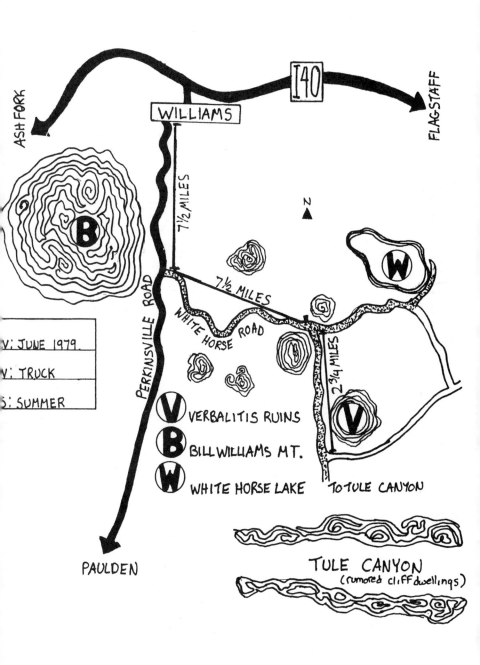

ASH FORK

I40   FLAGSTAFF

WILLIAMS

N

7½ MILES

B

W

PERKINSVILLE ROAD

7½ MILES

WHITE HORSE ROAD

2¾ MILES

V: JUNE 1979.

V: TRUCK

S: SUMMER

Ⓥ VERBALITIS RUINS

Ⓑ BILL WILLIAMS MT.

Ⓦ WHITE HORSE LAKE

Ⓥ

TO TULE CANYON

PAULDEN

TULE CANYON
(rumored cliff dwellings)

Verbalitis Ruin

㉓

10. Black Mesa Fossils

On a lighter note, I wonder if you have heard the one about the traveling trilobite and the farmer's bivalve mollusk?

Simply stated, the joke does not exist except in the mind of a perverted paleontologist. Anyhow, if you are one of those fossil hunters who can't take a joke and can't find a trilobite for the trees, you may want to try the limestone wells just east of Black Mesa in the canyon below.

It's no joke. There are plenty of fossils to be found here, and most can be located with little or no effort at all. I have seen trilobites plucked from the walls, as well as specimens of the rare horned coral.

Just keep your eye glued to the little black specks the size of a grade school eraser and you are on the right track. Removal is simple enough if you're equipped with a miner's pick and the strength of a three-year-old.

Now, if you are willing to take a risky climb, you may just find dinosaur remains higher up on the cliff walls. Make sure you are wearing hiking shoes and you are in good health. Mountains do hide their secrets, and Mama Nature makes it even more difficult to reveal them.

SPECIAL NOTES:

You're not going to believe this, but, there are things you can collect in Arizona that are neither illegal, poisonous or taxable. Fossils are one such item. Please don't tell the legislature.

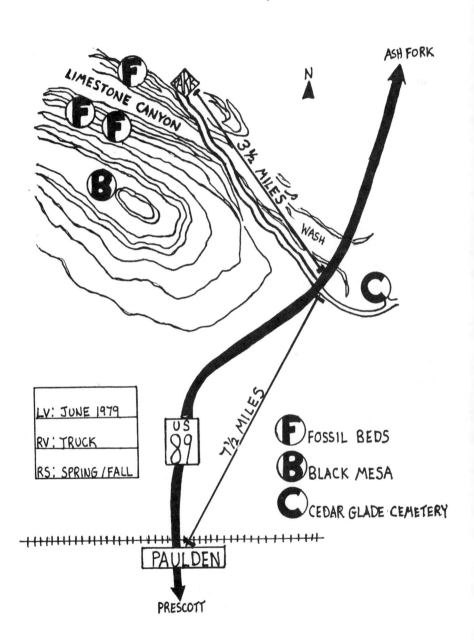

ASH FORK

N

LIMESTONE CANYON

F

F **F**

B

3½ MILES

WASH

C

LV: JUNE 1979

RV: TRUCK

RS: SPRING/FALL

US **89**

7½ MILES

F FOSSIL BEDS

B BLACK MESA

C CEDAR GLADE CEMETERY

PAULDEN

PRESCOTT

Black Mesa Fossils

11. Andy's Petroglyphs

While on our way to Walnut Canyon one day, we thought to explore the area round Wildcat Hill.

Years earlier, I had heard rumor of a cave and obsidian deposit that were supposed to exist on the east side and it was time to check it out.

At first, we came upon an old rock structure that was not of Indian origin, and a midden of beer bottles. Undaunted, we descended the north side where the mountain dipped into a canyon of sorts.

Here the walls were covered in petroglyphs—ancient writings the likes of which I have never before seen.

I have been taught by the sons of Hopi elders to read petroglyphs on a basic level. However, these did not fit the norm. While I have no idea how old they are, I would still assume these to have been drawn by the Anasazi who occupied this region some 700 years ago.

As for the cave, we did not have any luck. Perhaps you will fare better.

SPECIAL NOTES:

I have included an extra chapter at the end of this book which deals with reading petroglyphs. While it is by no means complete, it should still serve you as a guide to reading that which the archeologists claim no person can read. If they would only consult the Hopi....

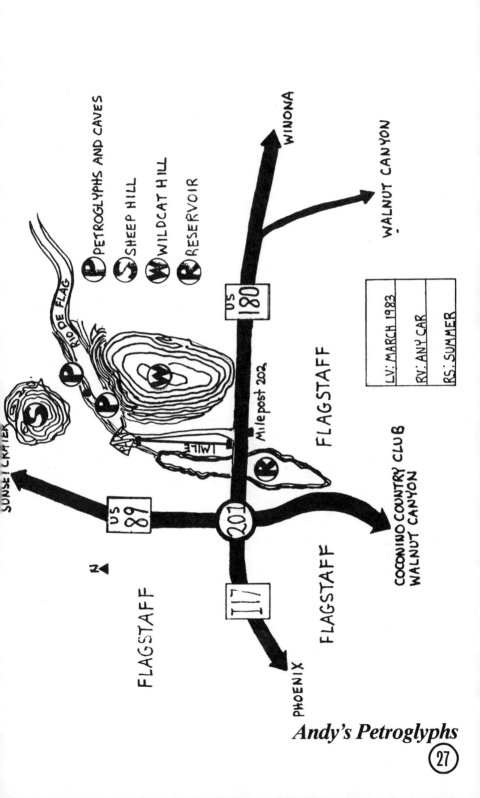

Andy's Petroglyphs

27

12. The Doney Park Ruin

From what I have been told, the Doney Park ruin was quite a puzzle for early archeologists. Built on the side of an ancient volcano cinder cone, almost every room has a small pit set in the middle of the floor.

It has been surmised that these were intended for storage. Yet, this phenomenon is not to be found in any other Sinagua settlement; at least, not in such abundance.

The ruin has been excavated, and I understand that it is privately owned. We were not disturbed while visiting the site, and there were no signs posted to discourage our entry.

Still, though, you should always be careful about inquiring into property ownership when you are unsure. Always ask for permission to cross or enter fenced property. To be careful means that you should not pick up any artifact, nor should you leave a contemporary artifact behind. We are talking about trash here.

SPECIAL NOTES:

You may have read *Explore Arizona*, my first book, in which I mentioned that the ice cave at Sunset Crater had been closed. Well, friends, the cave has been re-opened! Remember to take a flashlight and a crash helmet.

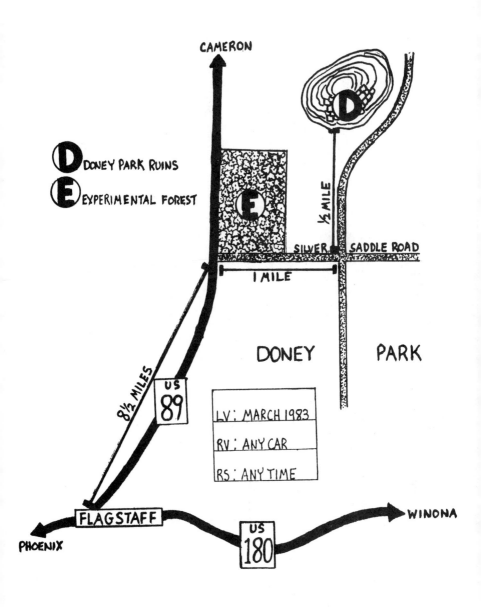

CAMERON

D DONEY PARK RUINS

E EXPERIMENTAL FOREST

½ MILE

SILVER SADDLE ROAD

1 MILE

DONEY   PARK

8½ MILES

US 89

LV: MARCH 1983

RV: ANY CAR

RS: ANY TIME

FLAGSTAFF

US 180

PHOENIX

WINONA

Doney Park Ruin

29

13. Cherry Canyon

I have always been particular when it comes to spectacular scenery, and I make it a point to chase down every lead that might present an opportunity for photographing.

Within the boundaries of Walnut Canyon National Monument, I went to look at a vista which had been recommended.

As it turned out, the view into Cherry Canyon surpassed all that I had hoped for.

They say that what is one man's meat is another's potato. You may agree when you look on Cherry Canyon. It is not the Grand Canyon, and it is not Bryce Canyon; the intricacies are not to be found here.

But, it is untouched and pristine, which is unusual for any natural reserve so close to civilization. Therein you find its beauty!

I would strongly urge you NOT to climb into the canyon, and I would strongly urge you NOT to touch any artifacts you may find here.

This is protected land, and the only reason it is still accessible is because no person has climbed into the canyon or distrubed the ruins. Please don't do anything that might close this area to others.

SPECIAL NOTES:

Whenever you are on federal property that has been made a national monument, remember that the government frowns on those who leave the designated trails.

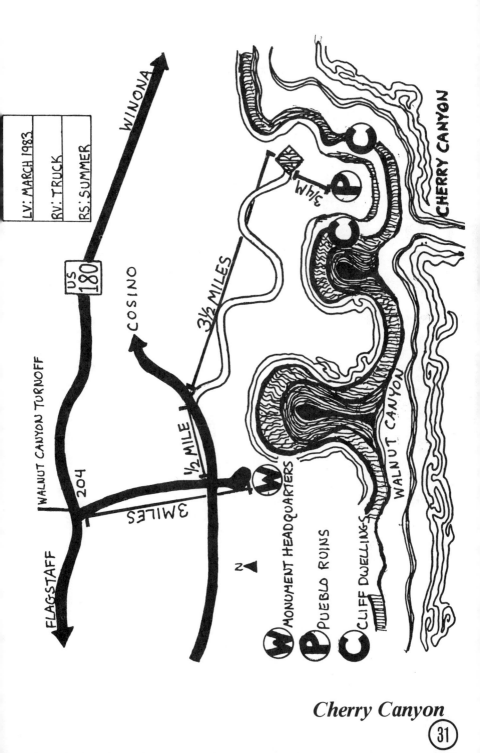

| LV: MARCH 1983 |
| RV: TRUCK |
| RS: SUMMER |

WINONA

US 180

COSINO

WALNUT CANYON TURNOFF

204

3½ MILES

½ MILE

3 MILES

FLAGSTAFF

N

3½ MILES

CHERRY CANYON

WALNUT CANYON

W MONUMENT HEADQUARTERS

P PUEBLO RUINS

C CLIFF DWELLINGS

Cherry Canyon

14. The Little Gary Ruin

Everyone needs a base when exploring the Arizona outback if they plan on staying in a certain area for two days or more.

The Little Gary Ruin was our base two years ago when we explored the Winona area for other ruins and rumored caves.

The Little Gary Ruin, while not one of the larger ruins in the area, has good level walls from which you can stretch a canvas tent and virtually create a covered room.

Here you can store your supplies, and from this ruin hike an easy ten miles in any direction and return by nightfall.

And, with few animals—both human and otherwise—in this area, your supplies should be safe when you leave camp.

If you decide to use the ruin, you might want to use our direction marks that lie just outside the north wall.

Three sets of rock arrows will point you in the direction of an obsidian dump that is two miles away, the collapsed roof of a lava tube five miles away, and a large ruin that is four miles distant.

Please don't move the markers!

SPECIAL NOTES:

Even though this ruin is not located on the reservation, it is still protected by law and no artifacts may be removed, except arrowheads.

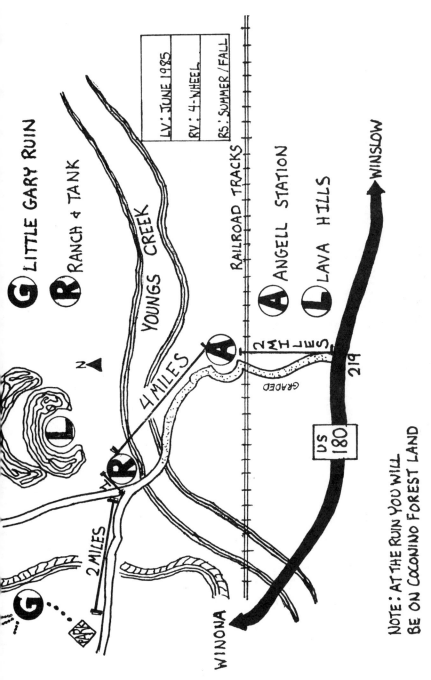

G LITTLE GARY RUIN

R RANCH & TANK

A ANGELL STATION

L LAVA HILLS

LV: JUNE 1985	
RV: 4-WHEEL	
RS: SUMMER/FALL	

RAILROAD TRACKS

YOUNGS CREEK

4 MILES

2 MILES

2 MILES

GRADED

2 MILES

WINSLOW

US 180

219

WINONA

N

PARK

NOTE: AT THE RUIN YOU WILL
BE ON COCONINO FOREST LAND

Little Gary Ruin

(33)

15. Homolovi

Just east of Winslow on a windswept bluff, you will find the ruin of Homolovi.

Once known as the most thoroughly "pot-hunted" ruin in Arizona, Homolovi is now finding new life and new meaning as it is transformed into one of the finest examples of archeological reconstruction work in the Southwest.

Since we last visited Homolovi, it has been designated a national monument.

Years ago, Homolovi looked like a bombed battlefield from the Second World War. Walls were unrecognizable; the only clue that it had once been a settlement came from the heaps of broken potsherds.

I was even told that pothunters came through the site with a backhoe!

Things have changed! The archaeologists are now busy at work reconstructing the fallen walls, putting in trails, and perhaps a museum to house what few intact artifacts they have been able to find remaining on the site.

SPECIAL NOTES:

Since Homolovi is now designated a national monument, arrowhead hunting is strictly verboten. Neither these or any other artifacts can be taken from the site.

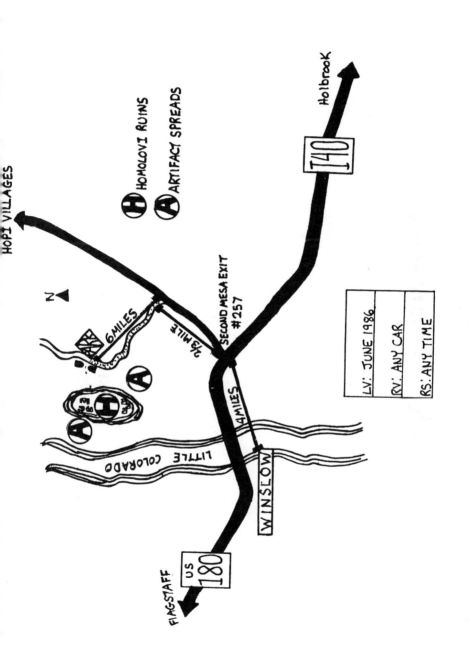

Homolovi

16. The Snowflake Pueblos

The area around Snowflake abounds in prehistoric ruins, most of which remain unexcavated.

The two ruins I have listed here have been excavated, but each new ruin turns up more and more arrowheads that are perfect for any collection. The artifacts, however, must be left where you find them.

The first pueblo (labeled "K" by the excavators) is the largest and contains nearly 500 rooms. It is here that you will find your best arrowheads.

The second pueblo is located on the old Carter Ranch, and may or may not be private property. We did find a "No Trespassing" sign, but portions of the fence that surrounds the ruin obviously fell years ago.

Exercise caution whenever you come upon a fenced area. Do not enter fenced property or where "No Trespassing" signs are posted. By law, the owner can prosecute for trespassing.

Many artifact spreads can be found along Hay Hollow Draw. The artifact law does apply here, but arrowheads are exempt.

Yet, if you are a collector of fossils, then Point Mountain Mesa is just for you. I have seen beautiful banded agates taken from its side, and these are usually found next to fossilized plant material. Crack out the slab of stone and pray for the best. You may even come up with a fish!

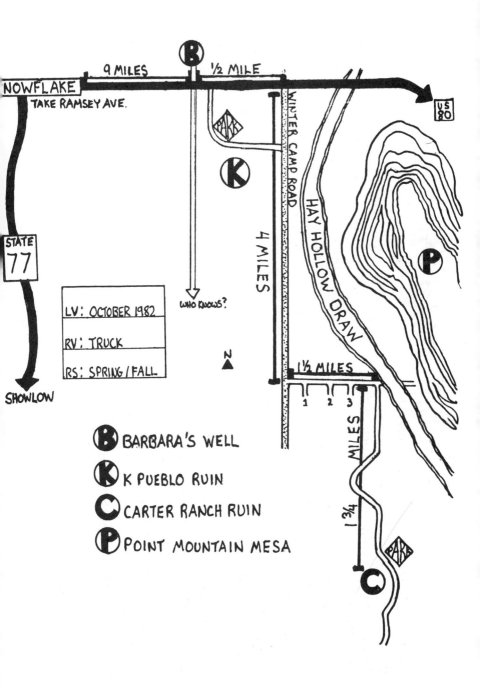

NOWFLAKE
TAKE RAMSEY AVE.

9 MILES

½ MILE

WINTER CAMP ROAD

HAY HOLLOW DRAW

US 80

STATE 77

PARK

K

4 MILES

WHO KNOWS?

LV: OCTOBER 1982

RV: TRUCK

RS: SPRING/FALL

N

1½ MILES

1 2 3

P

SHOWLOW

1 ¾ MILES

B BARBARA'S WELL

K K PUEBLO RUIN

C CARTER RANCH RUIN

P POINT MOUNTAIN MESA

PARK

C

Snowflake Pueblos

17. Harris Lake

Before I am accused of egotistically naming a site after myself, I should tell you that "Harris Lake" was so-named long before this "Harris" was born.

It is not one of your more-favored lakes in Arizona, but there is a mystery that surrounds it which I have been unable to solve.

According to the book, *Arizona Place Names*, there should be two huge subterranean caves next to the lake which served as prehistoric burial places.

Apparently, they were discovered earlier in this century. Friends of mine claim to have rediscovered them in 1981, but even though I have followed some pretty precise directions, I have been unable to locate them.

Perhaps you will have better luck.

All I know is that you are to draw an imaginary line between the radio tower and the highest point on a mountain northwest of the lake. At lake's edge you will find a boulder with a blue cross painted on it. We found that.

One quarter of a mile along the imaginary line after you leave the boulder, you are supposed to find a large opening in the ground just east of a large slab of rock. We did not find that.

We did find Harris Lake, though. It is more of a glorified cow watering hole than anything else. I do hope you find more.

SPECIAL NOTES:

I included this spot in my book for one reason only: it is my intent that you should have the thrill of discovery before I do.

Then, if you find the caves, drop me a line, in care of the publishers. I would appreciate it.

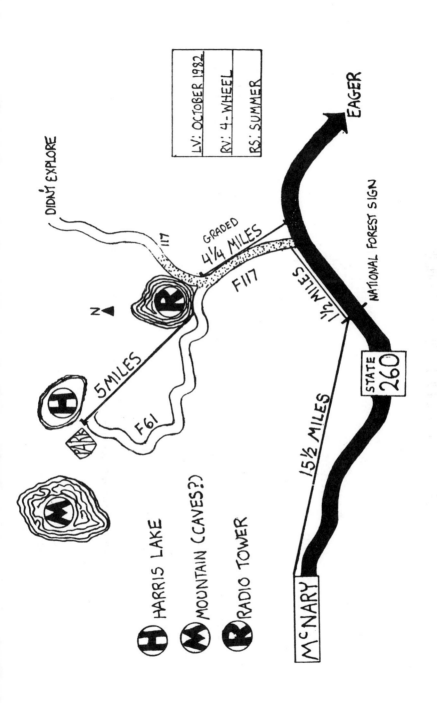

Harris Lake

39

18. Marijilda Nature Walk

I had been tricked into going up around Mt. Graham by some nature nut that told me Marijilda Canyon was loaded with Indian ruins. She even offered to drive, pay the gas bill, and feed me. I simply could not decline.

Well, there weren't any Indian ruins, no caves to speak of, no ghost towns, nothing but unspoiled nature.

We had a real blast watching two wild turkeys mate, seeing a wildcat chase a rabbit along the creek bed and witnessing the murder of one of those treasured red squirrels at the hands of what appeared to be a grey fox.

Red squirrels were all over the place, cow dung was all over the place, and there were no people to be seen any place!

Now, I didn't want to put some nature walk in my book; all I ever care about is finding something at the end of the road. Nevertheless, there are those of you out there who appreciate this sort of place, and you have told me so in your letters. So, now you have what you wanted.

If you happen to find any ruins in the canyon, please write to me in care of my publisher.

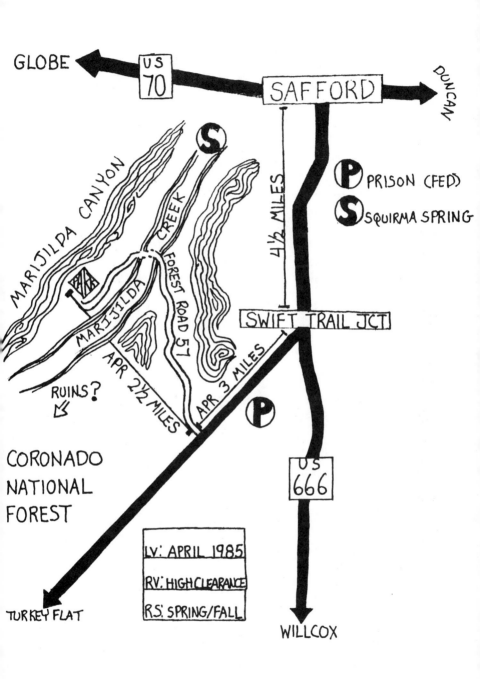

Marijilda Nature Walk

19. Diamond Point Crystals

Several weeks before writing this piece, a friend and I tripped down to Park and Swap in Phoenix so she could buy a pair of earrings. While perusing one of the various lapidary stalls, Bonnie came upon a table heaped with quartz crystals. The people who operated the booth told me they had been finding crystals at Diamond Point for years. That was all I needed to hear.

It was a couple of weeks later. I had almost forgotten about crystals when another friend came by and informed me that we had made plans to visit Diamond Point two weeks prior.

Alright, so I pulled out my copy of *Arizona Place Names*, checked the co-ordinates with a forest map, and off we were.

I will admit that once we arrived, we were disappointed. There were campers all over the blessed place, which led me to believe we were not about to find any crystals.

And then it happened that Pete found his first crystal in a gulley that ran off the mountainside. Soon, more were to be found. Wherever there was a runoff trail, there would be crystals.

I would recommend Diamond Point as a good spot to begin crystal hunting, if you are a novice, because finding them takes little effort and you don't have to free them from the surrounding rock.

As for other campers, they probably won't be looking for crystals, so don't let them bother you.

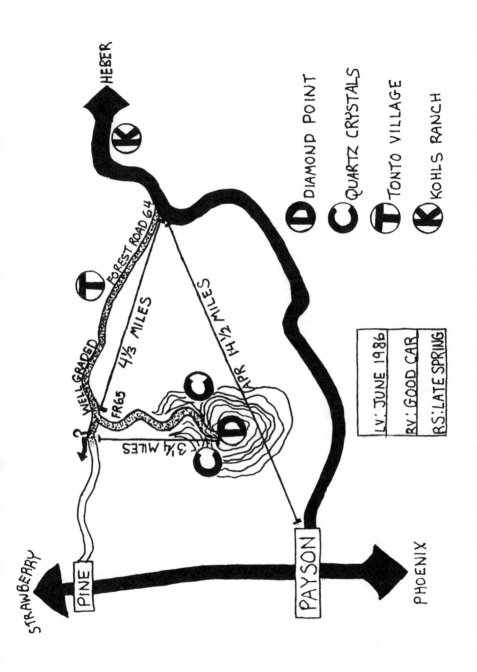

Diamond Point Crystals

43

20. The Grasshopper Ruin

Sometime around 1350 AD, the Anasazi of this region abandoned one of their largest pueblos, the one located at Grasshopper, and moved on.

Eventually, these people arrived at the Hopi mesas, but we still have no idea why they left Grasshopper. And, yet, if the mosquitos were as heavy then as they were when we visited, my guess would be that the entire village died of malaria and never went anywhere.

If you are up this way and you have several cans of insect repellent, you might want to check out this enormous ruin. We counted about 500 rooms that included a large kiva (the kiva being a religious gathering place).

Although the entire ruin has been excavated, you will still find enough multicolored pottery shards to give you some insight into the wealth of this culture.

There is little to be seen in the present poverty-stricken town that has emerged at Grasshopper. The poverty became quite apparent when several of the villagers asked us for money before we inspected "their" ruin. The giving of baksheesh is a tradition on the reservation, and even if they do not own the ruins you're looking at, it is in your best interest to pay them.

You would be surprised how much you can learn about their culture, and how much they are willing to open up for a couple of dollars or so.

I am sorry to remind you of this, but do not touch any artifacts you may find at this ruin.

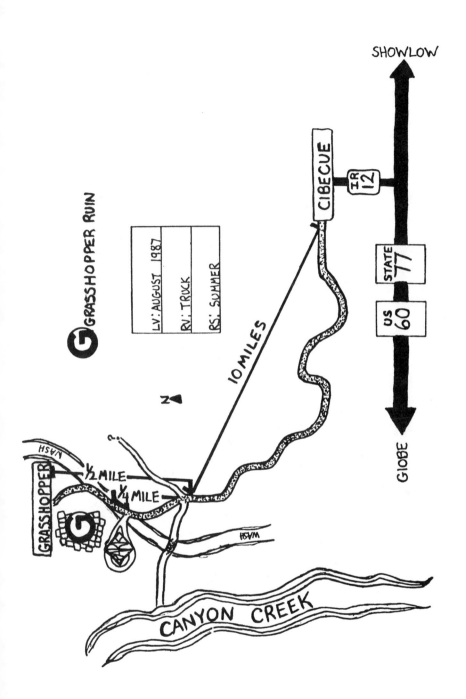

Grasshopper Ruin

21. Snake Rock

During the fall of 1986, when I first experienced the joy of autographing books, I must have met at least 30 people who actually complained about never having seen a rattlesnake.

Now, I can understand one being upset at having never seen the Grand Canyon or Meteor Crater. I can even understand why someone would be upset about HAVING SEEN that monstrosity in downtown Phoenix called Patriot Square.

Nevertheless, it is beyond me why anyone would want to come face-to-face with a rattlesnake.

With your requests in, I consulted the one person who would know where rattlesnakes could be found: Jeff Hauk. This guy has had more encounters with rattlesnakes than you and I have had with phone solicitors.

Years back, he and friend Kirk McRight found the perfect location for finding rattlesnakes. Although neither was bitten by the critters, I was warned that if I were to go out here with my luck I might as well count on becoming a statistic.

We had to go. Believing that wintertime would protect us from the hibernating rattlesnake, we decided to check it out.

Believe it or not, no sooner had we stepped from the van, a rattler decided to check us out. It did not run away like you see on nature films; this dude was on the attack. Later on, we figured out why.

As it was, Mike ran over another rattlesnake that must have been its mate.

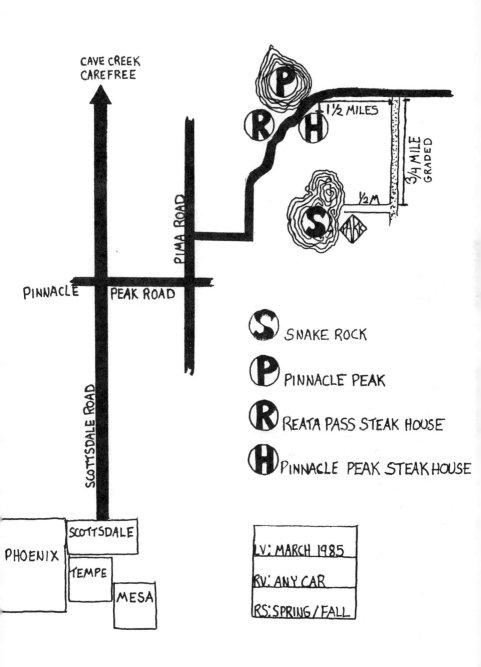

CAVE CREEK
CAREFREE

PIMA ROAD

PINNACLE PEAK ROAD

SCOTTSDALE ROAD

1½ MILES

¾ MILE GRADED

½ M

S SNAKE ROCK

P PINNACLE PEAK

R REATA PASS STEAK HOUSE

H PINNACLE PEAK STEAK HOUSE

LV: MARCH 1985	
RV: ANY CAR	
RS: SPRING / FALL	

PHOENIX

SCOTTSDALE

TEMPE

MESA

Snake Rock

47

22. *Four Peaks Amethyst Tour*

Let me start by warning my readers that the Four Peaks Amethyst Tour should only be undertaken by those who are familiar with the Four Peaks area.

This is quite important because it is just as easy to get lost here as it is in the Superstition Wilderness. The last thing I need is for a Search and Rescue team to find your body five miles from the designated trail; a copy of *Discover Arizona* clutched in your hand. Hey, it would give me nightmares!

For those of you who are familiar with Four Peaks, and who have braved that antithesis of chip-sealing they call a road, I am pleased to announce that we have found the amethyst mine.

And, guess what, it was close to Amethyst Spring on the topo maps. There was one drawback, however. The mine is fenced and posted with "No Trespassing" signs.

Not to worry, however. There are still plenty of outcrops in the general vicinity that hold a wealth of this prized purple gemstone.

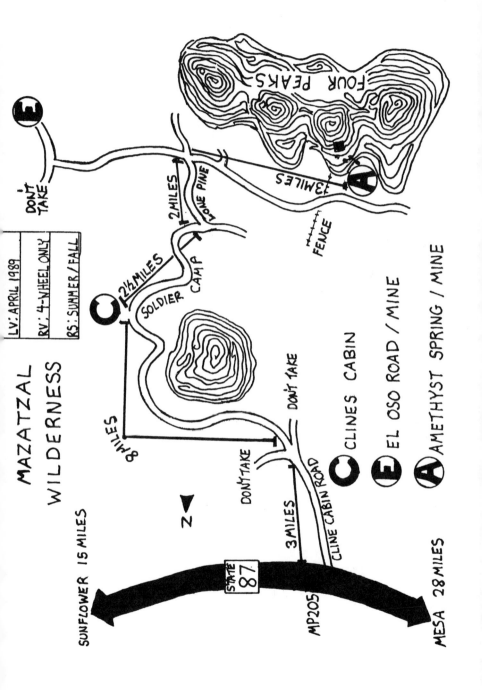

Four Peaks Amethyst Tour

23. The Lost Spanish Mine

Somewhere hidden deep within the mountains northeast of Carefree an ancient Spanish mine awaits discovery.

Could it be a lost trove of gold "Lost Dutchman" style? Or, is it just a figment of someone's imagination?

I really do not have the answer, but, one thing is for certain: the arristra stones used by the Spaniards to crush gold-and-silver-bearing-ore do exist.

I have seen them, and they lie all but forgotten in the canyon of Cave Creek.

Two years have passed since we last ventured up this way. Our original plan had been to enter the area in search of some medicinal herbs that are said to grow wild in these parts, especially by the stream bed.

Although a thorough search failed to turn up any of the herbs, we did find something even more intriguing—the broken arristra stones.

Why I have never heard about the lost mine before is a mystery to me. After all, the stones are there for anyone to see.

They are quite heavy and could not possibly have been carried in by man alone. Another peculiarity: the stones are carved out of a type of granite that is nowhere nearby.

These stones were important and they were brought here for an important purpose. We believe that if the mine does truly exist, it will one day be found on the heights above the canyon.

We never did make the hike; the sheer incline of the canyon walls make it quite impractical. Nevertheless, I am sure that one day it will be found.

SPECIAL NOTES:

From Carefree to Seven Springs there are many roads which will take you close to the interior, but just as many are barred to prevent trespassing.

Some mines in this area are still operating both legally and illegally. As I'm sure you can guess, the latter are usually guarded by weenies who do not care who or what they shoot. BE CAREFUL !!

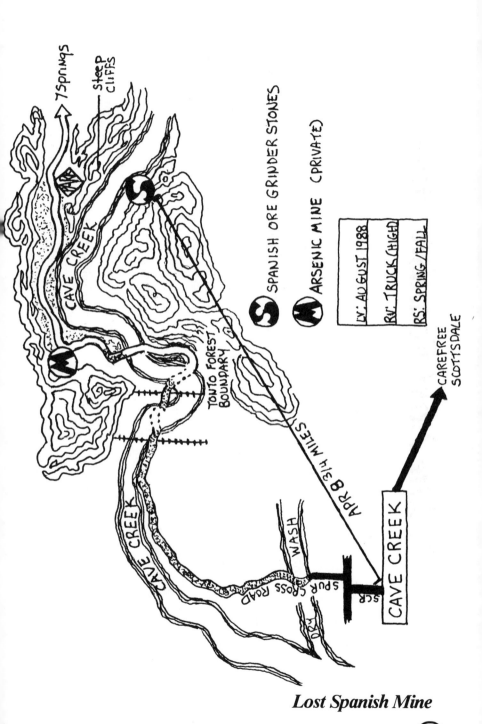

Lost Spanish Mine

24. The Medicine Wheel

While on an outing to the Verde River during my high school days, I told my tube-loving friends to drop me off where the "Park" sign is on the map.

I admit that I may have had a little too much to drink, otherwise I would have continued on with my companions. However, I saw the bluff to my side and was convinced there had to be a ruin on top.

I climbed the bluff alone and at first I did not find a thing. Okay, I have been mistaken before.

Then I noticed a large curiosity—two circles of stone, one inside the other.

It was large enough to be seen from the air. Was it an airline marker of sorts?

I really could not be sure, but small pottery shards in and about the circle convinced me that it had to be pre-historic.

I suppose I will never know why, but I decided to sit in the middle ring. Having read the Carlos Castaneda books, perhaps I thought it would imbue me with some power or something.

Honest to God, I had not sat in that ring for longer than five seconds, when I felt as though a cattle-prod had been put to my spine. I was out cold.

Years later, I told a Hopi friend about the experience and he informed me that what I had found was a medicine wheel which had been constructed to heal an ailing clan leader.

As for the ceremony used in conjunction with the wheel, that is lost in history.

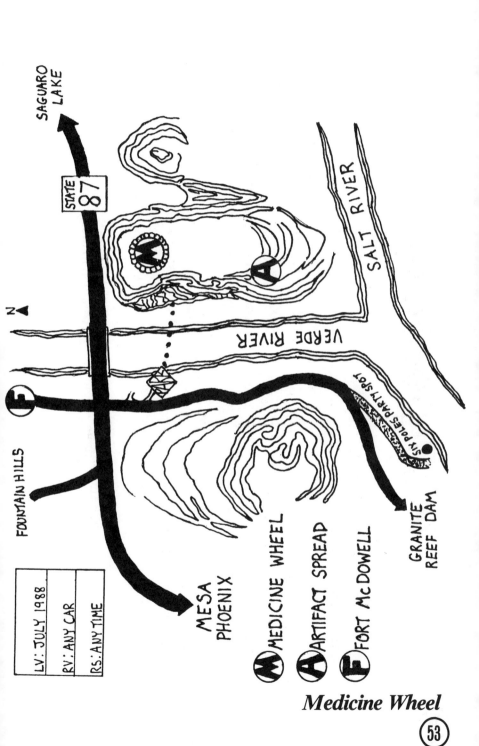

Medicine Wheel

25. Mesa Grande

Many years ago, a friend and I phoned the owners of Mesa Grande to ask their permission to dig.

Even though we offered to split the finds with them and do all the digging ourselves, they decided that excavation would best be left to the professionals.

Mesa Grande is the last unexcavated pueblo in the Salt River valley, an area once inhabited by the Hohokam Indians. Other than Mesa Grande and Pueblo Grande, the rest have been destroyed by farming and unbridled development.

Now, for the first time, archeologists will have the opportunity to excavate an untouched pueblo ruin, using present-day high-tech methods. This should give us a more complete picture of the Hohokam culture than we have ever had.

The ruin itself is fenced in to protect the site from looters. At the time of this writing, the mound must be viewed through the fence. Within the next few years, archeologists will be busy at work excavating and reconstructing.

Perhaps they will even build a museum that bears the names of those who made it all possible.

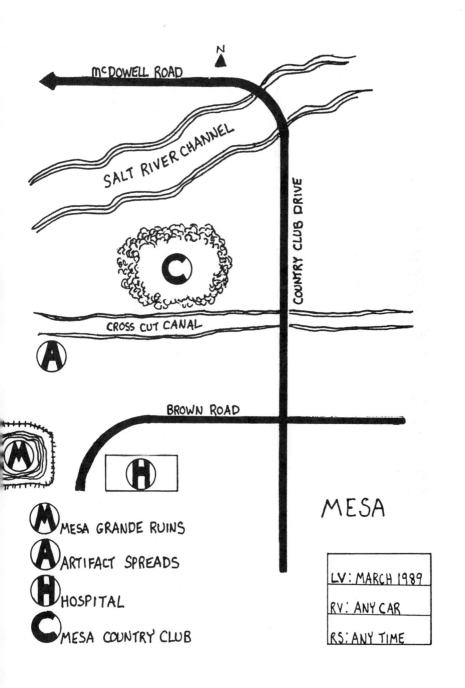

MESA

M MESA GRANDE RUINS
A ARTIFACT SPREADS
H HOSPITAL
C MESA COUNTRY CLUB

LV: MARCH 1989
RV: ANY CAR
RS: ANY TIME

Mesa Grande

26. Postma's Petroglyphs

One of the few people who have unselfishly granted me their time and the use of their vehicle has been Paul Postma.

Together with the renowned outdoorsman Dave Eichentopf, we have roamed this state and searched for a meaning to the petroglyphs.

Paul and Dave's favorite petroglyphs can be found in the White Tank Mountains. I have never seen such a great profusion of prehistoric writing anywhere in Arizona.

If you can stand the hike up this canyon, you will find walls that are entirely covered in petroglyphs.

What is strange, though, you cannot find a ruin on the surrounding cliffs, and there are no ruins in the immediate valley below. Farmers cannot even recall plowing up artifacts until you get clear to Litchfield Park.

To travel this distance and cover cliffs in petroglyphs would seem to indicate that the Hohokam had a special reverence for this place.

It is obvious from the small spring at ridge end that this spring probably provided water year round. Perhaps, then, in times of drought this may have been their only source of water. I do not know.

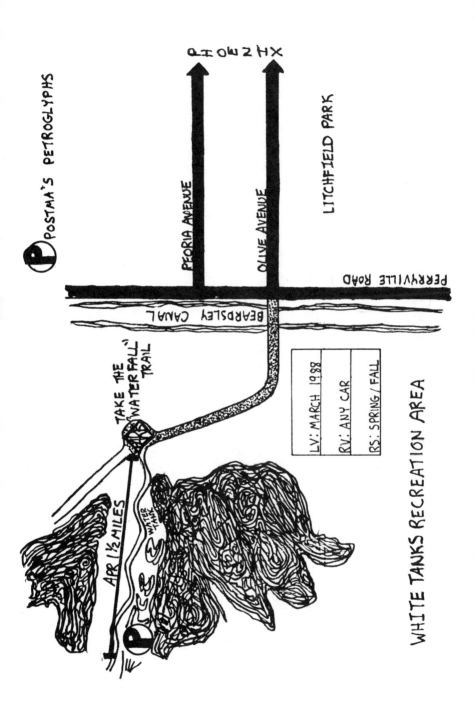

Postma's Petroglyphs

57

27. The Goodson Ruin

This, my readers, is the Goodson Ruin, named for its founder. Legend has it that Greg Goodson, having filled his body with a little too much liquid, went looking for some relief.

Exceedingly bashful, he decided to do his thing clear on the other side of a mountain. Rather than going around the mountain and having someone follow him, he chose to climb.

On top, he could not hold it any longer. Some say it was bladder pressure, but I do not think that was the case. I think he was gripped by excitement, the excitement of finding a huge, intact ruin!

It is a strenuous climb to the top. However, your efforts will be rewarded when you stand in rooms which can easily boast 900-year-old walls that have survived the onslaught of time. Some are even close to being six-feet tall.

Evidence at this ruin would suggest that it was built during a time the Hohokam faced the threat of invasion from more hostile tribes.

It is fortified, and the collection of arrowheads outside the walls would lead one to think that they may have been left behind after a war.

This is just speculation, however, but carbonized wood outside the fire pits and around the ruin would tend to confirm this conjecture.

SPECIAL NOTES:

All artifacts should be left where you find them, according to state law. Arrowheads are a different story.

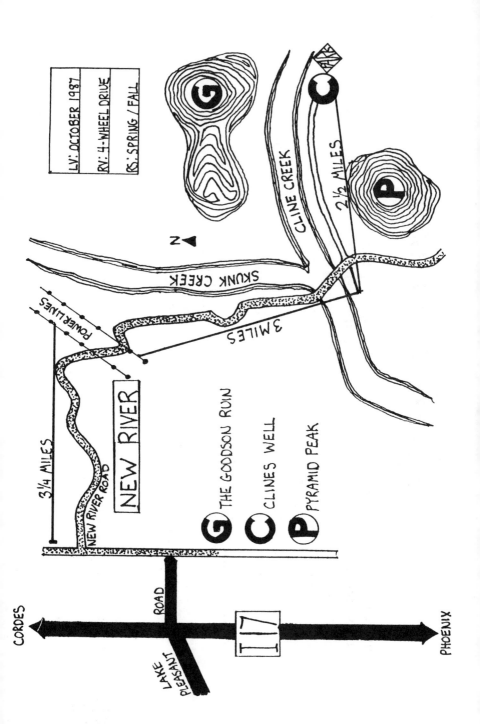

Goodson Ruin

28. Hot Springs Crystals

What is all the hoopla about these days over quartz crystals? I know that the New Age movement claims they give us all sorts of energy and supernatural powers, but let us see just how much energy they give you when you need to dig them out of solid rock!

You can believe in anything you want to, I suppose. One thing is for sure, there are quartz crystals to be found around Castle Hot Springs. You don't even need to take pick and hammer, because they litter the surface.

These will not be large crystals. At least, we have not found any large crystals. The place where we looked and where you will want to look is not in the stream bed proper.

Instead, focus all your attention on the runoff grooves in the slopes above the creek. The crystals are small and will be mixed in with a whole assortment of agates. Take along a metal detector and you might even stumble across a nugget or two, but do that in the creek. Be sure it is waterproofed.

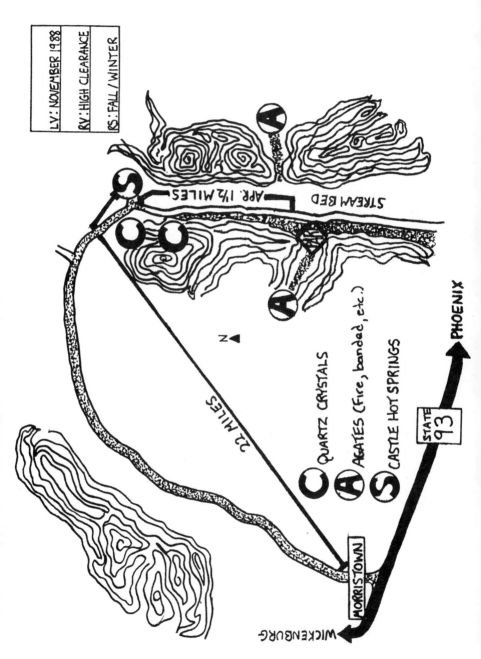

Hot Springs Crystals

29. Constellation (ghost town)

Opinions vary as to which is the best-preserved ghost town in Arizona.

Many people think of Jerome when asked to name the best, while others who obviously understand what the words "ghost town" mean, will tell you about Signal or Tip Top.

For years I could never make up my mind as to which was the best—Vulture City or Swansea.

Then it happened—Vulture was closed to sightseers, and the road to Swansea had been closed for repairs.

I had to have a ghost town, a real ghost town, not some place where people still live, like Jerome. I found Constellation.

Hey, I wasn't the first, okay, but at least I know I won't be the last. You people really have to see this place to believe it.

Just minutes after you leave Wickenburg, you will have your first encounter with a bygone town.

THERE ARE MINE SHAFTS EVERYWHERE (USE ALL POSSIBLE CAUTION! No mistake, MINE SHAFTS ARE DANGEROUS!), and the dumps are ideal for finding gem stones the miners did not care about.

Here and there you will see a building or two that may still hold antiques from early mining days. I doubt that anyone stops at these, though, because those who know about Constellation are in a great hurry to get there, forgetting about the trifles found along the way.

Constellation is a favorite haunt of local rockhounds. They try to keep this place a secret, and for this very reason, the buildings are for the most part intact. Sure, they have sustained damage from age and many have simply collapsed. As far as I am concerned, Constellation is the best town for the bucks.

SPECIAL NOTES:

MINE SHAFTS AROUND HERE HAVE A TENDENCY TO BE FLOODED AND TO COLLAPSE, especially after a rainstorm. These are NOT the kind of shafts you want to explore. I WON'T EVEN GO INTO ONE!

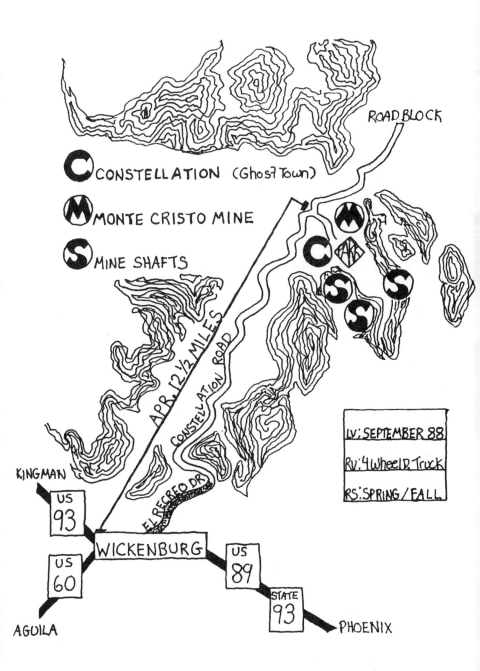

ROAD BLOCK

C CONSTELLATION (Ghost Town)

M MONTE CRISTO MINE

S MINE SHAFTS

APR. 12½ MILES

CONSTELLATION ROAD

EL RECREO DR.

LV: SEPTEMBER 88

RV: 4 Wheel Truck

RS: SPRING/FALL

KINGMAN

US 93

WICKENBURG

US 89

US 60

STATE 93

AGUILA

PHOENIX

Constellation (ghost town)

30. The Aguila Crystal Fields

I will admit that I am "into" quartz crystals, just like the rest of you. Although I have not found them to possess supernatural powers, they still hold an attraction—not fatal—but an attraction all the same.

Following the map out of Aguila, you will come upon a pass and a lot of white rock. You want to concentrate on the shadowed cracks, because that is where you will find the crystals.

While the crystals you find will be no longer than your middle finger, they are still of the variety that make handsome earrings and necklace pieces. People pay good money for the finished products.

BE CAREFUL! There are many mine shafts in the area which may or may not provide a yield of crystals. But be forewarned that these are the mine shafts that DROP STRAIGHT INTO THE EARTH. They are NOT side-bore.

And, if that will not convince you to stay away, you might want to talk to Billy Cope, a friend of mine who had his hand crushed in a mine up here. Rotten timber and falling rocks is all you need to remember!

SPECIAL NOTES:

There is an art to plucking whole crystals from the surrounding rock. Remember to pick at the rock one-inch below the crystals only after you have rubbed auto oil into the rock. Pick at the rock with patience.

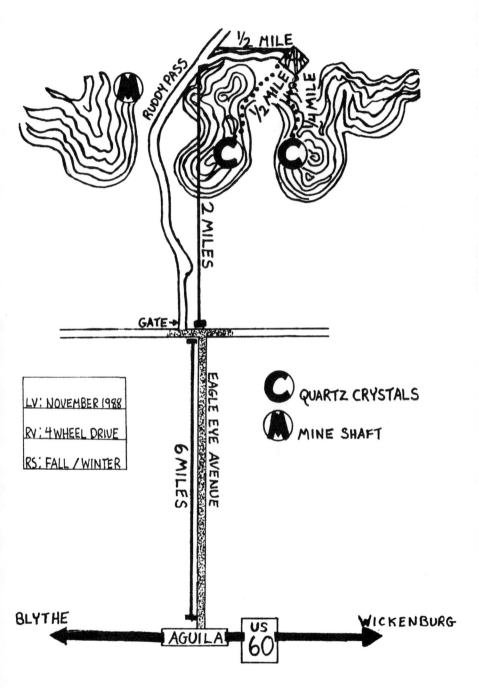

½ MILE

RUDDY PASS

2 MILES

½ MILE

¼ MILE

GATE →

EAGLE EYE AVENUE

6 MILES

LV: NOVEMBER 1988
RV: 4 WHEEL DRIVE
RS: FALL / WINTER

QUARTZ CRYSTALS

MINE SHAFT

BLYTHE

AGUILA

US 60

WICKENBURG

Aguila Crystal Fields

⑥⑤

31. Gordon's Garnet Patch

Ah, yes, the garnet! Akin to the ruby and often passed off as one, it is a valued gemstone and a name for some.

The fact is, it is about the only gem you will find with ease in the Arizona outback. There is a catch, though. There are only a few places left in Arizona where you can find them.

If you are looking for garnets, you may want to try the canyon east of Hell's Hole in the Crown King area. This is where we find "Gordon's Garnets." Ruby-red jewels, these garnets are highly-prized and sought after by rockhounds.

Look for the rock that is dark gray and sparkles like a snail track in the sun. Garnets are usually found in veins that lace this kind of stone. The garnets we found were slightly larger than a pencil eraser, but I am sure that larger ones can be found if you dig higher than six feet into the rock.

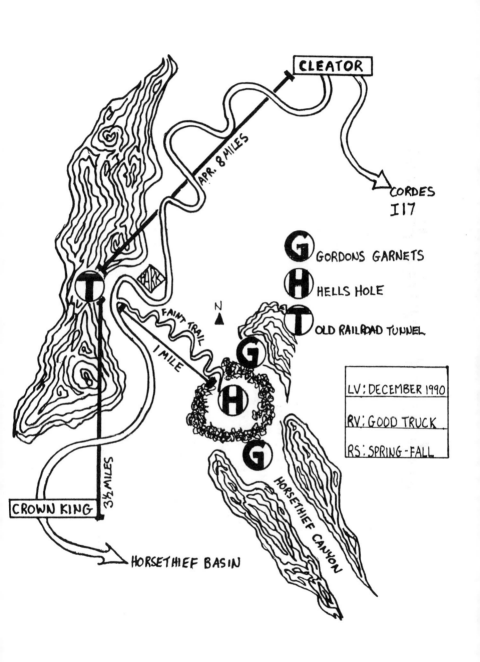

CLEATOR

APR. 8 MILES

CORDES
I17

G GORDONS GARNETS

H HELLS HOLE

T OLD RAILROAD TUNNEL

N

FAINT TRAIL

1 MILE

G

H

G

HORSETHIEF CANYON

| LV: DECEMBER 1990 |
| RV: GOOD TRUCK |
| RS: SPRING - FALL |

T

CROWN KING

3½ MILES

HORSETHIEF BASIN

Gordon's Garnet Patch

32. Crook Canyon

In my last book, Seven Springs was identified as the ideal place for skinny-dipping and diving in private. Since then, things have changed.

The swimming hole is now well-known, as twelve skinny-dippers we did not know will testify. Thus, it became obvious that we had to find another location for our naked activities.

Let it be known that we finally found the ideal location in Crook Canyon. It comes complete with river, and along its stretch there are an overabundance of pools which offer the perfect seclusion for those who wish to swim without the hindrance of clothes.

The vegetation is lush, much more lush than you will find at Seven Springs. You even have pine trees! There is a rapid current in the creek which prevents stagnation of the water.

And, this is rockhound country where you can find pyramidal fluorite and pyridoxel pyrite. The only drawback is—the road from Prescott to Crook Canyon is quite rough and should be traversed only in a four-wheel vehicle.

Once, while taking a shower beneath a waterfall in Crook Canyon, I was confronted by a large black-and-yellow-banded snake. I did not know if it was poisonous or not and I freaked. Since then, I have invested in a book, *Poisonous Dwellers of the Desert*. You may want to invest in a copy, too, because the reference might just save your life.

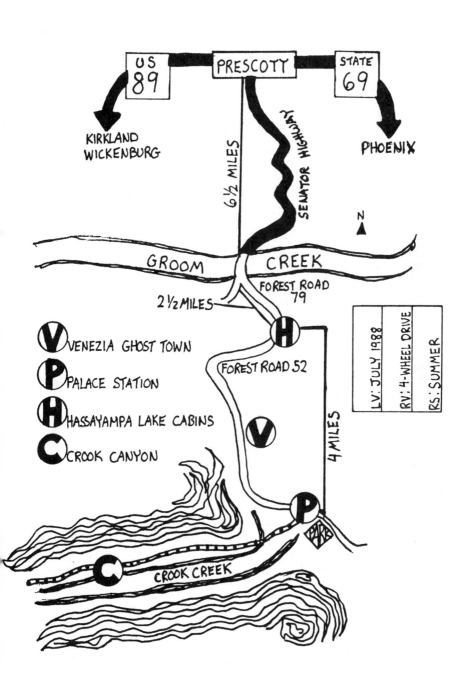

US 89 — KIRKLAND WICKENBURG

PRESCOTT

STATE 69 — PHOENIX

SENATOR HIGHWAY

6½ MILES

N

GROOM CREEK

FOREST ROAD 79

2½ MILES

V VENEZIA GHOST TOWN

P PALACE STATION

H HASSAYAMPA LAKE CABINS

C CROOK CANYON

FOREST ROAD 52

4 MILES

LV: JULY 1988 | RV: 4-WHEEL DRIVE | RS: SUMMER

PARK

CROOK CREEK

Crook Canyon

33. Clear Creek

Do you ever dream of finding the perfect camping spot? The kind of place where few people go on holidays and weekends, where you can swing from a rope on a tree into a crystal-clear swimming hole?

This location would have caves and cliff dwellings, streams and waterfalls, a natural environment that rarely knows of motorhomes and monoxide fumes. If you have ever dreamed of such a spot, I have found it at Clear Creek!

We love Clear Creek. For several years now, we have gotten the gang together in July and made our way to Clear Creek for a weekend of anything and everything you can think of.

Not one of us has ever gone away disappointed, because there is something here for everyone to do. We renew old friendships and breathe new life into the ones which have gone sour. That alone should tell you something about the magic Clear Creek has to offer.

I find the cliff dwellings to be my main interest; I love to poke around in ancient dwellings. Last time we were there, I strayed away from the cliff dwellings and located two prehistoric altars in the eastern draw.

I have been told they were used by the Two-Horn Society, a clan of the Hopi. Exactly how they were used remains another Arizona mystery.

You guessed it. Taking artifacts is a no-no.

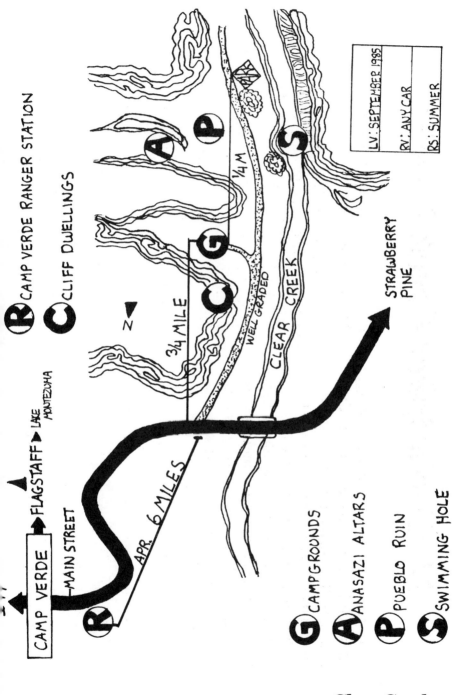

Clear Creek

34. Christopher Creek Fossils

In general, I try to avoid repeating sites that have been mentioned in other books. Well, Christopher Creek has been mentioned in quite a few books and it is easily found on any highway map.

However, while they talk about this being an excellent campground, as well as a fishing hole—neither of which is true—previous authors fail to tell you about the fossils to be found.

While vacationing on the rim, I decided to do a bit of exploring along Christopher Creek. I started out in hopes of finding signs of prehistoric Indian dwellings.

Instead, I found Christopher Creek to be one of the better untouched fossil beds I had ever seen. Oh, yeah, I did find pithouse ruins on the cliff which overlooks the fishing hole.

When it comes to fossils, you have to know what you're looking at, or else the encasing stone will appear to be nothing but stone.

In the dried-out portion of the creek, you want to take notice of the gray, unworn stone. This is primeval mud, and it holds the shell fossils that you are after.

Sometimes, if you are lucky, you will come upon stone that shows snail patterns or little dinosaur footprints. The luckier find whole bones.

I have never heard or seen people catching fish at Christopher Creek. The only thing anyone catches here is a cold. But don't take my word for it!

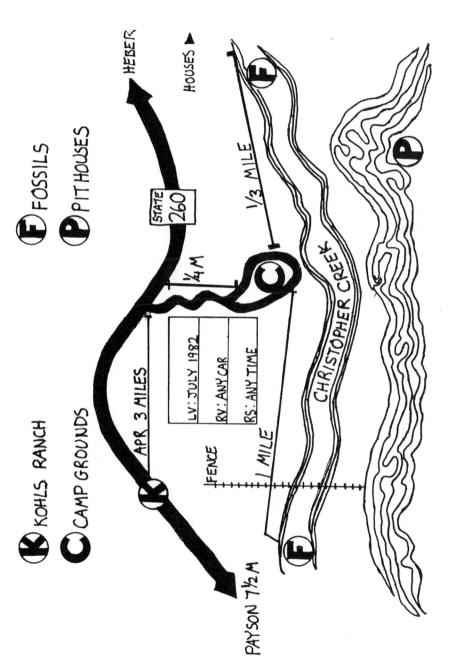

Christopher Creek Fossils

35. The Crack in the Rock

STARDATE: 2436. While orbiting the Verde Valley, we have encountered a force that seems bent on destroying our enterprise.

It is an alien force that will not allow the liquor store to open until 1200 hours. An "away" team has been dispatched to find something for the crew to do in the meantime. Their report follows:

The Crack is very difficult to find. You must follow the trail one mile out of the ranger station until you come upon the "Apache Maid" trail.

This will take you up into the mountains. Within another mile or so, you will see a water treatment plant. Start counting now.

Fifteen minutes along this trail, you will see a large crack that spans top to bottom of the rock. Opposite this crack, you start hiking down. At the end, you will find a fifteen-foot pool of crystal-clear water. Bring your swimming trunks. This is my favorite spot.

Capt. Rundle

STARDATE: 2436 sometime after 1200 hours. The crew seems to be enjoying this place. All of my crew have shed their clothing and appear to be swimming in water like we had on Earth.

I am not convinced this is water, though, and will descend to the same location to check out the surroundings in the same manner as my crew.

Capt. Harris of the starship "Scrog" signing off.

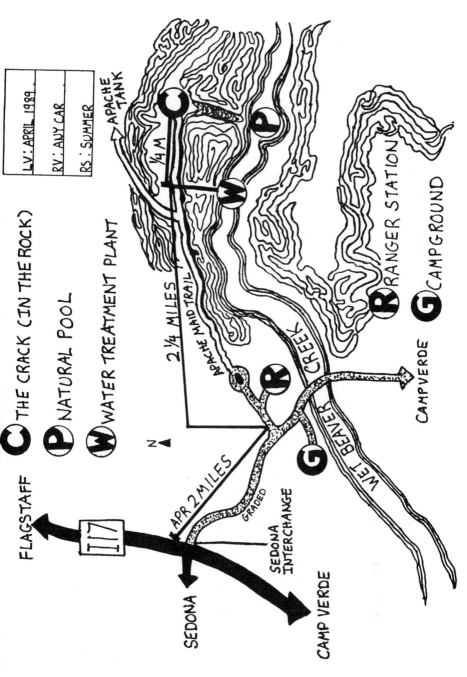

LV: APRIL 1989
RV: ANY CAR
RS: SUMMER

C THE CRACK (IN THE ROCK)
P NATURAL POOL
W WATER TREATMENT PLANT

APACHE TANK

¼ M

2¼ MILES

APACHE MAD TRAIL

N

R RANGER STATION
G CAMPGROUND

WET BEAVER CREEK

CAMP VERDE

APR 2 MILES

GRADED

SEDONA INTERCHANGE

I17

FLAGSTAFF

SEDONA

CAMP VERDE

Crack in the Rock

75

36. The McRight Ruin

Many years ago, when Darrell Duppa was trying to spell "Phoenix" and when Jack Swilling was trying to pronounce "canal," Angus McRight was saying, "Eureka, lassie, I have found the rainbow at the end of the pot."

True, he was a little high—on a hill, that is—and his discovery was a ruin that rivals Tuzigoot in size. Appropriately, it is called the "McRight Ruin."

Kirk McRight, descendant of the legendary Angus McRight, took me to the ruin which bears his uncle's name. I saw a ruin that remains intact, for the most part.

Even though it is within proximity to civilization, pottery abounds, as well as broken manos, axeheads and arrowheads, the last being the only artifacts that you can legally collect from the ruin.

SPECIAL NOTES:

Another side trip you may want to take will bring you to the mouth of Sycamore Canyon. This canyon has been virtually unexplored past the seven-mile limit.

I understand that the canyon is full of Indian ruins, as well as bears.

BE CAREFUL!

If you decide to investigate this area, I would suggest, for the first and last time, that you take along a rifle.

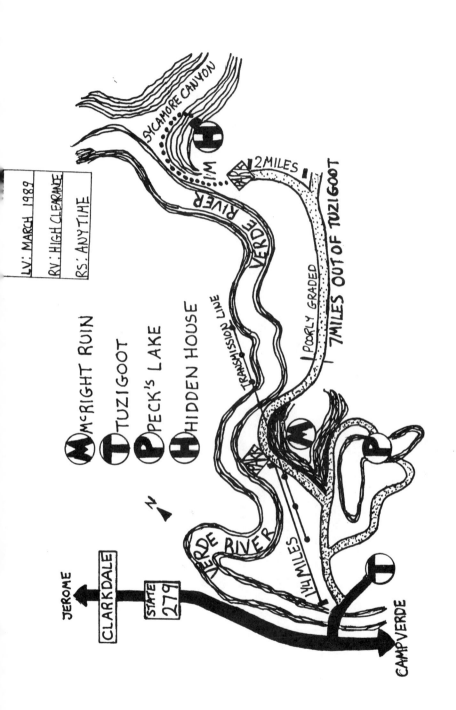

McRight Ruin

37. Ft. Grant Massacre Site

One of the more tragic episodes in Arizona history occurred just across the creek from the site of Fort Grant.

Remarkably, the cavalry was not involved in this massacre of innocent men, women and children. This time, murder was carried out by the residents of Tucson, Mexican nationals and a handful of Papago Indians.

The victims were Apaches who had lain down their arms.

Apaches waiting for internment were met in the night by drunks who had mistaken them for MARAUDING Apaches. This was a vengeful kill.

If you were an Apache in territorial days, peaceful or not, you were earmarked for death!

However, these peaceful Indians, and the manner of their deaths, sparked a great deal of outrage. Martial law was almost imposed in Arizona as a result.

In the end, the culprits were given a trial and acquitted. A perfect example of justice, 1871 style!

Nothing remains of Ft. Grant today. However, artifacts from the fort's history can still be found between the highway and the San Pedro River.

The massacre site is in doubt. Nevertheless, the symposium of 1878 did declare that the massacre occurred on the bluff that has been noted on my map.

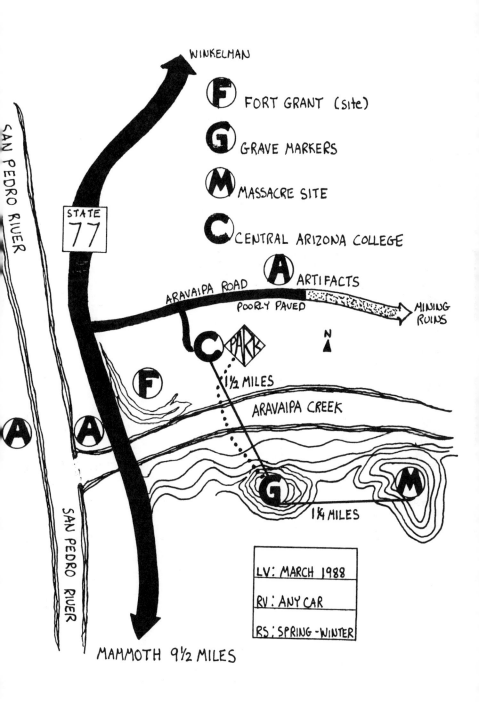

WINKELMAN

F FORT GRANT (site)

G GRAVE MARKERS

M MASSACRE SITE

C CENTRAL ARIZONA COLLEGE

A ARTIFACTS

SAN PEDRO RIVER

STATE 77

ARAVAIPA ROAD

POORLY PAVED

MINING RUINS

N

C PARK

1½ MILES

ARAVAIPA CREEK

F

A

A

G

M

1¼ MILES

SAN PEDRO RIVER

LV: MARCH 1988

RV: ANY CAR

RS: SPRING - WINTER

MAMMOTH 9½ MILES

Ft. Grant Massacre Site

⑦⑨

38. The Southern Belle Mine

It was hot. We were sweating like prepubescent pigs and our beer supply was gone. Paul wanted to turn back, Dave wanted to turn back and I wanted to turn back.

We couldn't, though. I forget how we had gotten this far in the first place.

I had been told that finding the Southern Belle Mine was like looking for a virgin in a whorehouse. Nevertheless, we managed to find the trail.

Hours away, we found the fossilized cliff. We also found a nut with a gun, so be careful.

DO NOT HIKE TO THE MINE ITSELF! VISITORS ARE UNWELCOME!

Instead, concentrate on the fossilized shelf, because that is really why you are here.

Fish fossils are jam-packed in the cliffs. I have looked elsewhere for the same, but this mountain is the grand-daddy of them all. Take your pick, pick slowly, and you won't be disappointed.

SPECIAL NOTES:

FOSSIL ALERT, FOSSIL ALERT! We drive through blasted hills all the time. Simply pull off to the side of the road whenever you pass through a multicolored highway cut. The fossils are there.

Of course, you should be careful of traffic. Nevertheless, cars or no cars, there are many discoveries that await the adventurous.

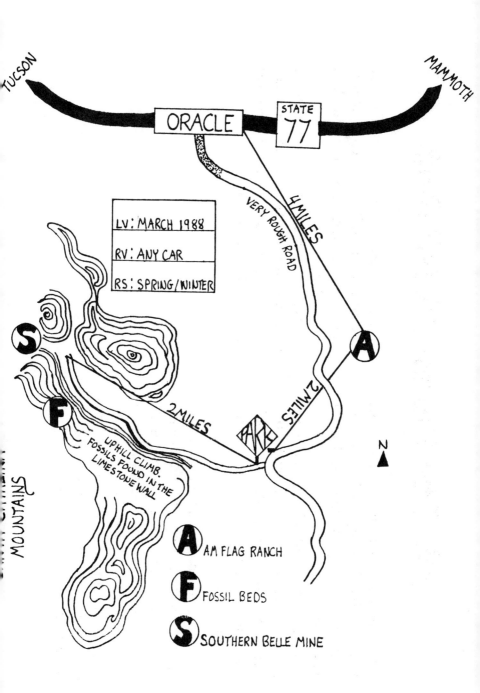

TUCSON

MAMMOTH

ORACLE

STATE 77

VERY ROUGH ROAD

4 MILES

LV: MARCH 1988

RV: ANY CAR

RS: SPRING/WINTER

S

F

2 MILES

2 MILES

MINE

N

UPHILL CLIMB. FOSSILS FOUND IN THE LIMESTONE WALL

MOUNTAINS

A AM FLAG RANCH

F FOSSIL BEDS

S SOUTHERN BELLE MINE

Southern Belle Mine

39. The Zamar Fossil Beds

Weathered rock formations are your best bet when looking for fossils, gemstones, or anything else that a rockhound may want.

And, guess what? The Zamar Fossil Beds are located along a huge rock formation. No mine shafts, no hassle, just a lot of fossils that await the sound of your pick and shovel.

Now, if you have a trailer home or a good-sized tent, come out and spend a week. There is no one around for miles. Privacy and fossils are guaranteed, as well as a hell of a good time.

This only applies to rockhounds, however. If you are not a rockhound, we have names for people like you.

Are you "into" Apache Tears? Fan out just south of the hills and keep your eyes glued to the ravines. This is the best place to find them.

Also, if you like pyrites, you may want to check out the area around a small Indian ruin that is just west of the lower hills. The ruin is "clean."

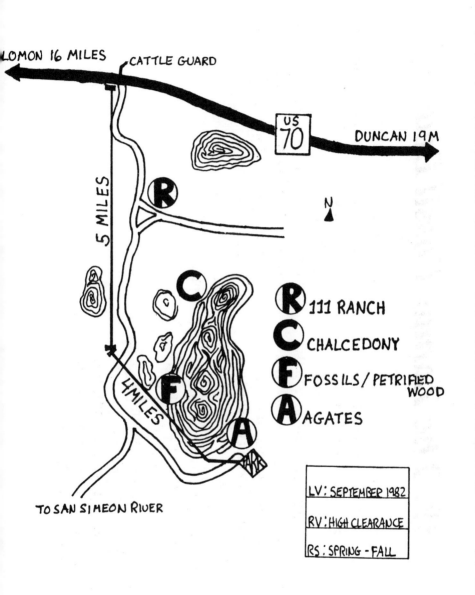

LOMON 16 MILES CATTLE GUARD

US 70

DUNCAN 19 M

5 MILES

N

R 111 RANCH

C CHALCEDONY

F FOSSILS / PETRIFIED WOOD

A AGATES

4 MILES

TO SAN SIMEON RIVER

LV: SEPTEMBER 1982

RV: HIGH CLEARANCE

RS: SPRING - FALL

Zamar Fossil Beds

83

40. *The Geronimo Surrender Site*

A sad part of history was written on September 4, 1886. This was the day when the Apache "Patton" formally surrendered to the United States government.

This is where Geronimo stood. It is the site where he symbolically signed away his hatred for those who destroyed his people. And, when you stand before the rockpile that is his only monument, you stand where the proudest of men once stood.

Here, you will feel the grief that he once felt for having finally given to the white man all that no man should ever own—the whole of a people.

It is a lonely valley, this valley of Geronimo. I have never felt too comfortable here, because I feel some guilt for what my own ancestors may have done to the American Indian.

When you drive in, you want to look for the corrals. The site is slightly west of these. A large ruin overlooks the site and remains unexcavated. In this ruin and all others, you may take nothing but arrowheads.

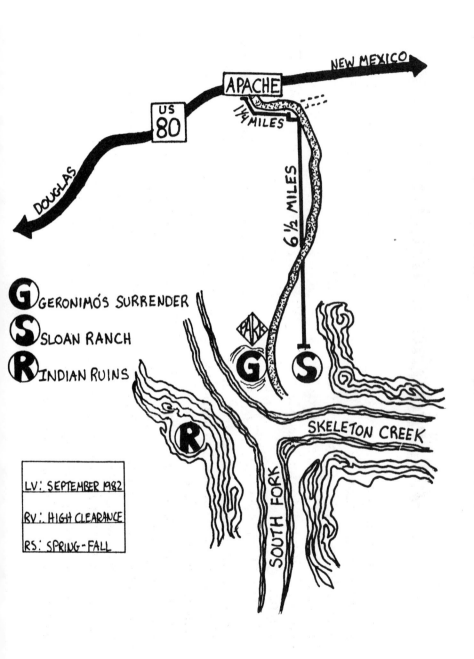

NEW MEXICO

APACHE

US 80

1¼ MILES

DOUGLAS

6½ MILES

G GERONIMO'S SURRENDER

S SLOAN RANCH

R INDIAN RUINS

G

S

R

SKELETON CREEK

SOUTH FORK

LV: SEPTEMBER 1982

RV: HIGH CLEARANCE

RS: SPRING-FALL

Geronimo Surrender Site

41. Marble Canyon

With the price of quality marble being so high today, and knowing that a lot of stone sculptors would give their eyeteeth for the location of a free source of marble, I decided to include Marble Canyon.

There is enough here for everyone.

This is an abandoned quarry that offers stone for statues, paving and architectural cosmetic work.

Even the photographer will have his or her day taking shots of what appears to be some strange, ancient temple left by stone-worshipping Druids. There are very few trees around.

When we last visited the quarry, it was unoccupied. My BLM maps also show it to be located on state property. I would take that to mean it is still not privately owned.

HOWEVER, IF SOMEONE INSISTS YOU LEAVE, I WOULD ADVISE YOU TO DO SO!

This quarry still contains a number of pre-cut slabs which are found at the bottom and which might pose a problem when you try to remove them.

Be careful when going down and try to go in from the rear.

EVEN THOUGH YOU SEE RAIL-INGS, THEY ARE RUSTED THROUGH AND ARE QUITE UNSAFE. DO NOT USE THEM!

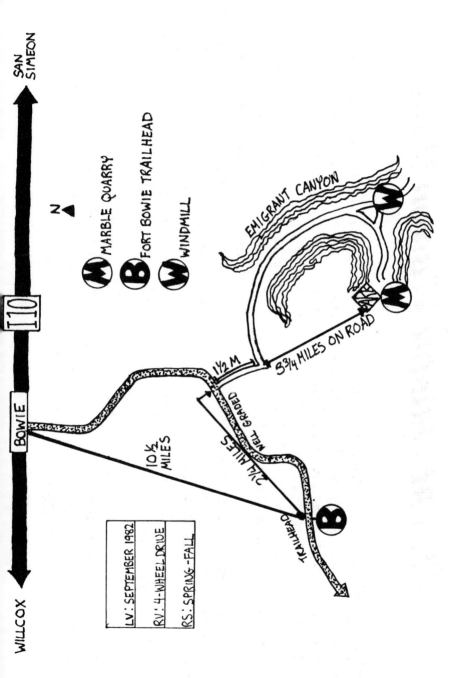

Marble Canyon

87

42. The Quiburi Mission Ruins

Once you have seen one Kino mission, you have seen them all. That is what I used to think when taking friends to San Xavier del Bac.

Funny, old Xavier is not even the most historical mission he set up, and still people flock to it. Few realize that Quiburi was his first.

If a little hike doesn't bother you, and mosquitos are little nuisance, you may want to check out this mission. It was the first one established by Europeans in North America. Guevavi once had that distinction—until archeologists and historians were able to date Quiburi as having been built some three years earlier. In 1697, this was the good Father's birthday child.

Quiburi is a ruin and not a fully-restored tourist trap. If you are one who likes worthless trinkets, you do not want to come here.

However, the history buff will find walls that are still erect, mounds where the Presidio once stood, and plenty of colonial artifacts. These must remain where you find them. The mission site is privately owned.

SPECIAL NOTES:

The adobe ruins of Contention City are on the other side of the San Pedro River. This is where you want to use a metal detector. While I have never discovered anything of value at the site, my friend has a twenty-dollar gold piece that says different. If you find one, you owe me a beer.

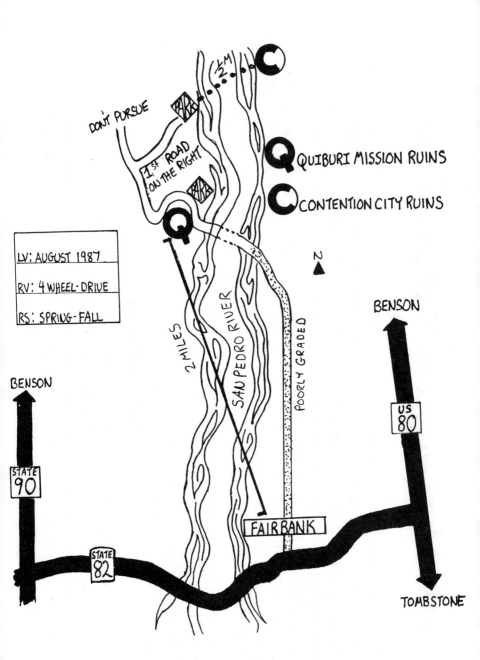

DON'T PURSUE

1st ROAD ON THE RIGHT

2¼ MI

QUIBURI MISSION RUINS

CONTENTION CITY RUINS

LV: AUGUST 1987

RV: 4 WHEEL-DRIVE

RS: SPRING-FALL

BENSON

2 MILES

SAN PEDRO RIVER

POORLY GRADED

N

BENSON

US 80

STATE 90

STATE 82

FAIRBANK

TOMBSTONE

Quiburi Mission Ruins

43. The Guevavi Mission Ruins

Most hiking books refer to the mission ruin as being the site of the ghost town, Calabasas. The fact is that the town of Calabasas disappeared from the face of the map more than fifty years ago.

Guevavi, however forgotten, still remains. Nevertheless, you may not enter the ruin itself.

Guevavi was established by Father Eusebio Kino a few years prior to 1700 and abandoned a few years after the founding of San Xavier del Bac.

Today, the ruin is fenced in and privately owned. From what I understand, there is an archaeological dig presently taking place at the site.

Artifacts can be found outside the fenced area along the Santa Cruz sandbanks. These have been known to include arrowheads—the only artifacts you can legally collect from this site.

SPECIAL NOTES:

I have been told by other people who explore this region that a forgotten mission ruin can be found just west of here.

A library research project led me to conclude that this cannot be true; all of the known Kino missions have been located. However, it is possible that another missionary founded a mission in this area.

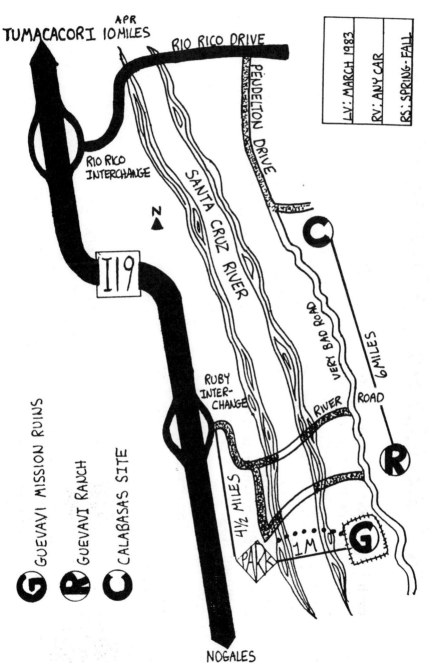

TUMACACORI 10 MILES

RIO RICO DRIVE

PENDELTON DRIVE

APR

RIO RICO INTERCHANGE

N

I19

SANTA CRUZ RIVER

RUBY INTER-CHANGE

VERY BAD ROAD

6 MILES

RIVER

ROAD

C

R

4½ MILES

PARK

1 M

G

NOGALES

LV: MARCH 1983	
RV: ANY CAR	
RS: SPRING - FALL	

G GUEVAVI MISSION RUINS

R GUEVAVI RANCH

C CALABASAS SITE

Guevavi Mission Ruins

91

44. Las Guijas Petroglyphs

If you are interested in petroglyphs, and your physical condition is tip-top, you should look into these writings. To get there requires the best hiking shoes.

I reached the top in a pair of K-Mart specials. The difference in the price bought the gas it cost to get up here.

I should tell you that I have found NO ruins around Las Guijas Petroglyphs. This appears to be a recording spot for the spiritual.

Once on top of the main mountain, you will find migration symbols without the personal identity markings of the Hopi clans. I would surmise that they viewed this particular site with some amount of reverence, for you see that nothing indicates territorial design.

If you read the petroglyphs long enough, you will understand.

You also have a ghost town nearby. It is indistinct, as most ghost towns are. Hollywood portrays ghost towns as being complete towns with a little decay. Do not ever be fooled by this illusion.

This is Mr. Arizona speaking, and I am here to tell you that ghost towns in this state consist of foundations, mounds of rubble and a few well-picked-over buildings.

It is not what you see on television westerns.

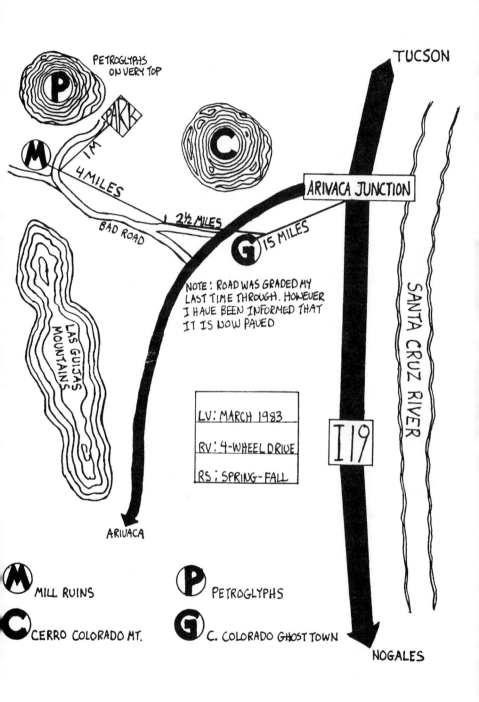

Las Guijas Petroglyphs

45. Martinez Hill

For almost a century, the weekend archeologist would call Martinez Hill his or her home. Then, as fate would have it, Martinez Hill was listed as an historical monument.

This means that you must have a four-year degree to legally dig at the site. Hey, boys and girls, it is time we all go to the University of Arizona to legally dig in a prehistoric garbage can!

Remember when I said that there are few fortified Hohokam settlements left untouched and unexcavated?

Martinez Hill is one of them. And, what makes this place even more significant is that Spanish trade beads can be found in the ruin. Obviously, Father Kino and his followers made their way to the Hill.

When last we visited this spot, Mike Biewener and I parked in the wash just north of Stock Road. Here we found quartz crystals in clusters.

They are small, mind you, but could still make a great addition to your rock collection. There was also fire agate but not jewelry material.

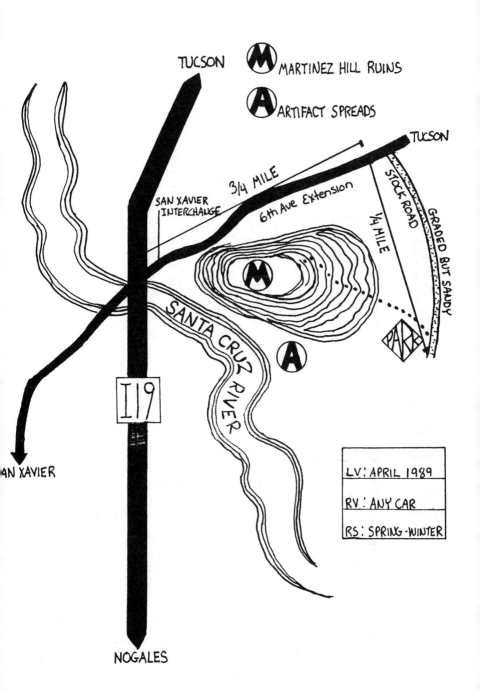

TUCSON

M MARTINEZ HILL RUINS

A ARTIFACT SPREADS

TUCSON

3/4 MILE

SAN XAVIER
INTERCHANGE

6th Ave Extension

STOCK ROAD

GRADED BUT SANDY

¼ MILE

M

A

SANTA CRUZ RIVER

I19

PARK

SAN XAVIER

| LV : APRIL 1989 |
| RV : ANY CAR |
| RS : SPRING - WINTER |

NOGALES

Martinez Hill

95

46. The Rillito Artifact Spread

In *Explore Arizona!* I gave my readers the locations of several artifacts spreads in the vicinity of Firebird Lake.

I am pleased to report that my last visit confirms that these sites remain intact. There was an archaeologist friend who worried that people might "rape" these sites, but they did not.

Therefore, I am going to give you another fantastic artifact spread. I do hope that it is appreciated and that this same appreciation is extended to the area around Rillito.

Mike and I accidentally stumbled upon this site while we were looking for an old, abandoned mine. It was supposedly loaded with smoky topaz crystals. We never did find the mine.

We believe the sites on the map were once prehistoric production areas. This assumption is based on the fact that both show a high concentration of chert and obsidian chippings. There are even un-finished manos and stone rings.

It is obvious that neither site has been excavated. In that case, you must leave any artifacts you find lying right where you found them.

A HEFTY FINE AWAITS THOSE WHO DISREGARD THIS WARNING!

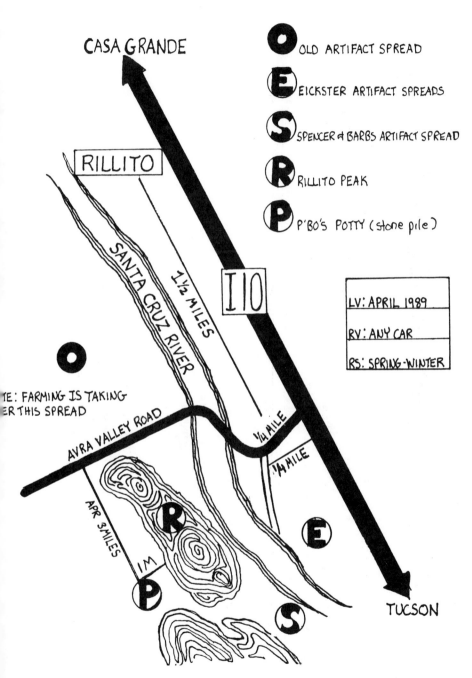

Rillito Artifact Spread

47. The Biewener Agate Claim

Mike Biewener is a man who has gained high respect among his fellow rockhounds because he has the uncanny ability to find your proverbial needle in the haystack.

Without any training, only experience, he can find the most precious of Arizona gemstones with little effort.

The Biewener Agate Claim is not a formal claim, but it is his pet discovery. He is more than willing to share its location with you.

Agate types that I have never seen outside of Alabama can be found in these mountains. However, only the trained eye will have the luck of discovery.

Most of what you find will be stones that are perfect for use in a rock tumbler. They are hard to cut and almost impossible to facet. And yet, if it is the raw beauty of multicolored gemstones that attracts you, it will be a field day.

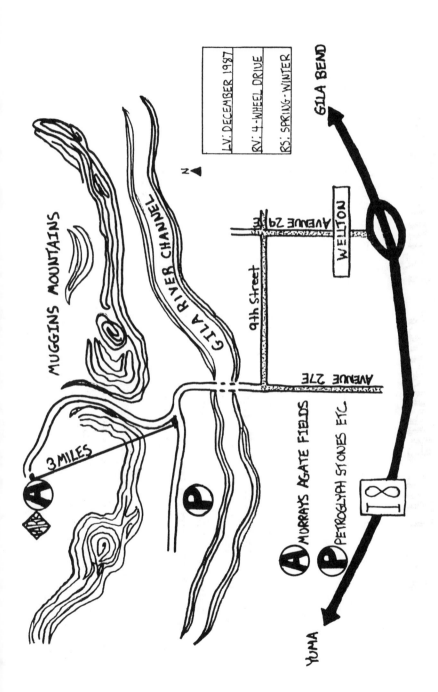

Biewener Agate Claim

48. The Laguna Gold Placers

I am not a real enthusiast about this part of the state because it is just too damn hot for me. So, if you ever wonder why I write so little about this area, you have your answer.

However, I have listed three sites in and around Yuma that you may find interesting.

I am somewhat glad I have explored this mini-Sahara, because we found a good area for gold placers. We even found a bit of gold!

If we had been equipped with more than a few gold pans, I am sure we would have found a lot more gold. So much for hindsight.

When you reach the riverbank that is indicated on the map, keep your eyes open for black sand. The reason that black sand is important to the gold hunter lies in the fact that gold tends to accumuate at the bottom of these deposits which are mainly iron in composition. Gold is a heavier metal than iron, so it tends to sink beneath it.

SPECIAL NOTES:

If you manage to find a spot that is laden with gold, you can file a mining claim in Arizona.

Keep it a secret, though, and dig and sift to your heart's content.

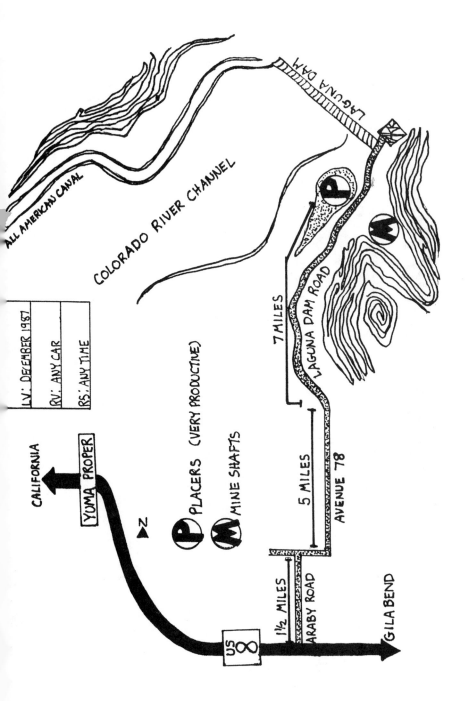

Laguna Gold Placers

49. Castle Dome Geodes

Damned Castle Dome! Wherefore art thou, Castle Dome? A touch of old Will seems appropriate because we were stranded here by some girl named Juliet.

That is how we found the geodes.

I think it could not go without saying that I was one pissed-off Romeo who would have died in that forsaken place if she had not come back five hours later with a case of beer and a tear in her eye.

The beer would have sufficed.

I swear to you that the Castle Dome Mountains are Satan's playground. If you do not carry enough drinking water with you, you will start seeing swingsets that are not there. To this I attest.

However, if you bring enough water, you will be seeing geodes. I guarantee they are there.

BE CAREFUL, not only of heat prostration, but OF DIRECT-DRILL MINE SHAFTS, as well.

They can be found anywhere in this area, and they go straight down into the earth!

Few have been blocked or fenced, SO BE EXTRA CAUTIOUS.

Also, there are thousands of rusted nails across from the cemetery, which assure the sandaled tourist of a trip with tetanus if he or she happens to step on one.

Old miner shacks still hold antiques for the collector, and your metal collector can go wild just south of the cemetery. Yes, old coins and other relics have been waiting for you to claim them.

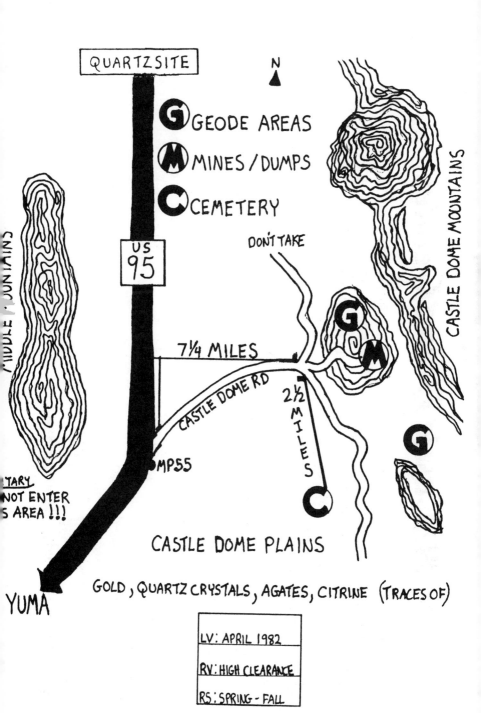

QUARTZSITE

N

G GEODE AREAS

M MINES / DUMPS

C CEMETERY

US **95**

DON'T TAKE

7¼ MILES

G
M

CASTLE DOME RD

2½ MILES

G

MP55

MIDDLE MOUNTAINS

CASTLE DOME MOUNTAINS

TARY
NOT ENTER
S AREA !!!

C

CASTLE DOME PLAINS

YUMA

GOLD, QUARTZ CRYSTALS, AGATES, CITRINE (TRACES OF)

LV: APRIL 1982

RV: HIGH CLEARANCE

RS: SPRING – FALL

Castle Dome Geodes

50. Ha-Au-Kee Artifact Spread

Recently, *Explore Arizona* went into its second printing, but not without certain changes. All but one of my artifact spreads had to be deleted, along with other sites, and replaced.

It seems that a few people chose not to heed my warnings about artifacts and they took a lot more than arrowheads from these sites. Authorities from the Gila River Reservation requested that these hikes be removed at the next printing.

Now, we all must pay the price: we are banned from poking around in these areas without tribal permission.

You really can't blame them. Still, I am convinced that there are those of us who have a respect for the past and for civilizations that came before. Therefore, I will include one last artifact spread in this book.

Again, pay attention to the fact that you may take nothing more than arrowheads from this site. Although it is not on a reservation, the law still applies.

Ha-au-kee is an artifact spread situated in the plaza that was once a very large Hohokam community. You will find pottery types from almost every period of Hohokam history and even a few pieces of Sinagua black-on-white that suggest trade.

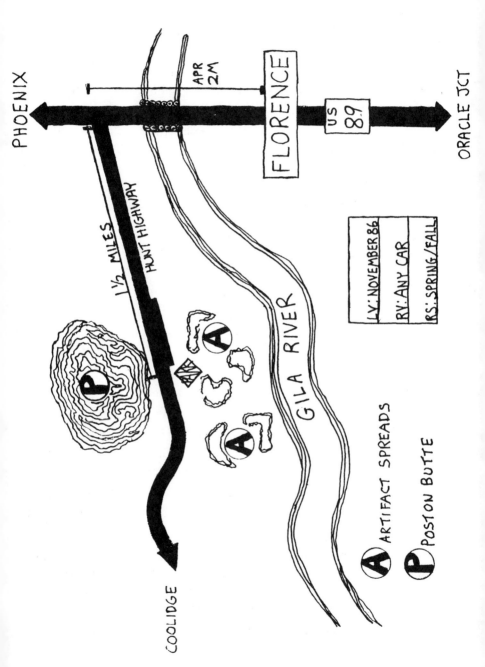

Ha-Au-Kee Artifact Spread

Appendix

While you endeavor to "discover Arizona," you may find that certain permits and licenses are required to visit various parts of our state.

For example, several of the Indian nations in Arizona request that you acquire a special use permit before hiking into remote areas of their land. Also, the state of Arizona requires you to purchase a permit before you fish or hunt.

Therefore, I have listed the phone numbers of various tribal and state agencies which control the distribution of these permits and licenses. Remember to tell them the purpose of your visit, when you would like to go, when you plan to leave, and request information about local laws and regulations. (All numbers use 602 prefix.)

INDIAN NATIONS		U. S. FOREST SERVICES	
Hopi	734-2441	Coconino	556-7400
Navajo	871-4941	Coronado	670-4552
San Carlos Apache	475-2653	Kaibab	635-2681
White Mtn. Apache	338-4364	Prescott	771-4700
Tohono O'odham	383-3286	Tonto	225-5200

Arizona State Game and Fish Department 942-3000
Topographical Maps: Wide World of Maps 279-2323
To report archaeological vandalism 1-800-VANDALS

Meet the Author

Rick Harris, encouraged by the success of his first book, *Explore Arizona*, has compiled a second series of fantastic places to discover Arizona.

The result is *Discover Arizona*, whose pages include Harris' comments and detailed maps to guide adventurous explorers to fifty more hidden and out-of-the-way places in Arizona.

For years, the author, a native Arizonan, and his friends, have enjoyed these secluded spots around the state. They frolicked among ancient ruins, cliff dwellings and old forts, skinny dipped in azure pools, flirted with waterfalls, and discovered crystals, fossils and arrowheads.

Rick Harris, combining his interests in art, archaeology and nature, has followed up on leads furnished to him by friends and readers of his first book so you, too, can *Discover Arizona*.

Reading Petroglyphs

In order to read the petroglyphs, you need to know how the messages are structured. If the petroglyphs seem to run in one single line, then read them from right to left. Group petroglyphs are altogether different and must be read as though you were reading into a spiral. Start from left to right, then follow any discernible lines—that is, compatible glyphs—until you reach the center. Happy hunting!

Bear Clan	Badger Clan	Parrot Clan	Eagle Clan
Spider Clan	Fire Clan	Snake Clan	Water Clan
Bow Clan	Coyote Clan	Rabbit Clan	Butterfly Clan
Cloud Clan	Side Corn Clan	Kachina Clan	Sun Clan
Hawk Clan	Crow Clan	Tobacco Clan	Pumpkin Clan
Large Reed Clan	Small Reed Clan	Two Horn Society	One Horn Society

Clan Leader   **Deceased Clan Leader**    **Individual**   **Settlement**

Directions    **Spring (water)**   **Water**    **Good Soil**

Bad Soil   **Corn**   **Sun**   **Moon**

Planting Time   **Hunting**   **Good**   **Bad**

Destruction   **Rebuilding**   **War**   **Brotherhood**

Excess Food   **No Food To Give**   **Life**   **Death**

Burial   **Spirit**   **Past**   **Present**

Turtle

Owl

Macaw

Sheep

Bear

Fish

Elk

Deer

Turkey

Mountain Lion

Beaver

Scorpion

Rattlesnakes

Rain

Disease

Birth

Enemy

Friend

Marriage

Family

Migration

Shield

Atlatl

Peaceful

Open Shelter

Trade

No Trade

Mesa

Blankets

Pottery

Cloud

Star

Supernova

Rainbow

Index of Places

(Numbers refer to page numbers.)

Outdoor Books from Golden West Publishers

CACTUS COUNTRY

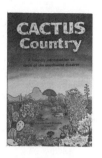

Before you touch, read this fascinating book on cactus of the southwest deserts. The many illustrations and humorous cartoons make this trip through the desert one to remember! *Cactus Country* by Jim and Sue Willoughby.

5 1/2 x 8 1/2—112 pages . . . $6.95

SNAKES and other REPTILES of the SOUTHWEST

This book is a must for hikers, hunters, campers and all outdoor enthusiasts! More than 80 photographs and illustrations in the text and full color plate insert, this book is the definitive, easy-to-use guide to Southwestern reptiles! *Snakes and other Reptiles of the Southwest* by Erik Stoops and Annette Wright.

6 x 9—128 pages . . . $9.95

HIKING ARIZONA

50 hiking trails throughout this beautiful state. Desert safety—what to wear, what to take, what to do if lost. Each hike has a detailed map, hiking time, distance, difficulty, elevation, attractions, etc. Perfect for novice or experienced hikers. *Hiking Arizona* by Don R. Kiefer.

5 1/2 x 8 1/2— 160 pages . . . $6.95

EXPLORE ARIZONA!

Where to find old coins, bottles, fossil beds, arrowheads, petroglyphs, waterfalls, ice caves, cliff dwellings. Detailed maps to 59 Arizona wonders! *Explore Arizona!* by Rick Harris.

5 1/2 x 8 1/2— 128 pages . . . $6.95

ARIZONA OUTDOOR GUIDE

Guide to plants, animals, birds, rocks, minerals, geologic history, natural environments, landforms, resources, national forests and outdoor survival. Maps, photos, drawings, charts, index. *Arizona Outdoor Guide* by Ernest E. Snyder

5 1/2 x 8 1/2—128 pages. . . $5.95

ORDER BLANK

GOLDEN WEST PUBLISHERS

☼ 4113 N. Longview Ave. • Phoenix, AZ 85014

602-265-4392 • **1-800-658-5830** • FAX 602-279-6901

Qty	Title	Price	Amount
	Arizona Cook Book	5.95	
	Arizona Crosswords	4.95	
	Arizona Museums	9.95	
	Arizona—Off the Beaten Path	5.95	
	Arizona Outdoor Guide	5.95	
	Arizona Small Game & Fish Recipes	5.95	
	Cactus Country	6.95	
	Chili Lovers Cook Book	5.95	
	Cowboy Slang	5.95	
	Discover Arizona!	6.95	
	Explore Arizona!	6.95	
	Fishing Arizona	7.95	
	Ghost Towns in Arizona	5.95	
	Hiking Arizona	6.95	
	Prehistoric Arizona	5.00	
	Quest for the Dutchman's Gold	6.95	
	Snakes and other Reptiles of the SW	9.95	
	Verde River Recreation Guide	6.95	
	Wild West Characters	6.95	
Add $2.00 to total order for shipping & handling			$2.00

☐ My Check or Money Order Enclosed......... $

☐ MasterCard   ☐ VISA

Acct. No.   Exp. Date

Signature

Name   Telephone

Address

City/State/Zip

Call for FREE catalog

Discover

3/93   MasterCard and VISA Orders Accepted ($20 Minimum)

This order blank may be photo-copied.